The 10 Rules of Empowerment

By Carlos Silva

ISBN 978-0-692-13617-1

www.10empowermentrules.com
10empowermentrules@gmail.com

DEDICATION:

To Michelle, Brandon, Melissa, and Bryan, may the wisdom in this book inspire and empower you.

Special dedication to my grandfather, Elias Cruz. His passion for books and the wisdom they contain influenced me to develop that very same love.

ACKNOWLEDGEMENT:

A very special thank you to Kevin. For being a great friend and encouragement. Your enthusiastic support, comic relief, and our lively conversations helped to keep me going on this journey of discovering and writing about the truths of Empowerment.

CONTENTS

Introduction

It is my hope that you have chosen to read this book because you believe that life is intended to be a journey of self-discovery and continual growth. In other words, a journey of self-empowerment.

Empowerment is the process of gaining knowledge that leads to right thinking, producing right actions, resulting in right outcomes. Self-empowerment should be our most lofty goal. As each of us has been designed with that one common purpose; To become the best and brightest version of ourselves. And for this task we are all uniquely qualified. Yes, your best self, your Empowered Self is who you are purposed and destined to be.

We all have this inner longing to be GREAT…to be recognized, to feel important and appreciated. This is not foolish pride. It is a desire that is "built in" to each of us. It is by discovering your Empowered Self that you are able to realize this inner longing.

Also keep in mind that in life, you have an audience. Yes, you are on a stage and your audience is everyone that you interact with in your personal and professional circles. Your audience is your wife, husband, kids, mother, father, sister, brother, boss, co-workers, etc.

This audience of yours also wants to see you at your very best, at your highest potential. They want to be inspired and impressed by YOU. They are secretly cheering you on. They want and deserve to see the best version of you. Your Empowered Self.

Listen, there is much in this life that can disempower us. That can cause us to feel victimized, powerless, and hopeless. The circumstances of daily living can often press on us in ways beyond what we can bear. Denying us our divine birthright to control and direct our lives towards the most positive and productive ends of our own choosing. Additionally, it is true that much of our own thinking and "mental programming" also serves to keep us in a powerless and victimized state.

When we rightly understand basic empowerment concepts, we can take back control and become more masterful in our daily living. No longer a leaf in the winds of life, mercilessly tossed this way and that. We can now become more present, purposeful, and powerful. In our thoughts, feelings, words, actions, and results.

It is a key premise of this book that in this life we are not victimized by any force other than ourselves. And this book is intended to offer principles, concepts, and practical habits that will enable you to uncover and realize your inner champion, Your Empowered Self.

The 10 Empowerment Rules presented in this book are not original, they have existed, dare I say, from the beginning of the human experience. I am confident that your own life experiences, plain sense, and intuition will validate them as truth

In the pages that follow you will find many positive precepts that will serve to enlighten, encourage, and inspire you. So, make sure to read through the entire book. This book is intended to be a lifelong companion. Because every time you pick it up and read it, it will provide you further understanding and insights into the many wisdoms it contains.

I invite you to step forward on the wonderful and exciting journey of empowerment. Of realizing the fullness of your potential in every area of your life. Of discovering Your Empowered Self. I promise, your life will never be the same.

Cheering you on!!!
CS

You Are AMAZING and UNIQUE

Before we begin our empowerment conversation I want to start with a compliment. Because it is important for you know that you are AMAZING and UNIQUE.

This is not an empty compliment, but a statement of fact. There is wonder and beauty in all the created order, but it is abundantly clear that at the pinnacle of all creation, human beings stand tall as it's crowning achievement. Yes, the human being is the most complete and complex creature in all of the created order. Your body and mind have no parallel. And furthermore, in this amazing package of marvelous, individual human creation there lies a perfectly unique identity and personality that will never, ever be duplicated. Yes, you are AMAZING and UNIQUE.

That is your compliment to start of this book. You are welcome. And now.... Welcome to our Empowerment conversation.

Not only are you AMAZING and UNIQUE, but have you stopped to consider that you live in a world that is CUSTOM made for YOU?

Every creature is perfectly suited for the environment which it inhabits. Fish have gills so they can survive underwater, birds are engineered for flight. Bats have sonar, etc. Human beings are also perfectly designed to be able to survive in our environment. We do not need to wear special space suits or apparatus.
This environment is perfectly suited for us. We do not need special training or unique tools to be able to survive day to day. We simply live our lives. Yes, we are perfectly designed to live in this "made for us" environment.

But we are designed to do much more than just survive. We are also designed to THRIVE in this environment. We are the only beings in the universe that are perfectly suited for all that exists in this world. Because we have been endowed with unique talents and capabilities that allow us to fully utilize all that this "made for us" world has to offer.

Just like our bodies are specifically designed to perform the life functions necessary for our survival in this environment. The world was also intentionally designed to allow us to REALIZE and MATERIALIZE all that we can imagine. The universe was designed for US. For us to bring forth all that we desire from it.

Consider our cities, towns, highways, and skyscrapers. Have we not brought all these forth from this environment? Have we not harnessed the power of the wind, water, the sun, electrons, plants, animals, etc.? Have we not conquered gravity, outer space, underwater, underground, the mountains, the oceans, etc.?

Yes, we have subdued this world and have fully subjected it to our creative and imaginative will. And, the world has been a most willing subject. And this is because it was made for this very purpose. To be the medium by which intentional and purposeful beings can bring forth and make real their intentions and desires. This world is perfectly designed for us and we are perfectly designed for it.

The Strawberry

Consider the simple strawberry. Why does it exist? The all too obvious answer is....it must exist for our pleasure and enjoyment. Because we have the eyes to see its beautiful red color and distinct shape. We can smell and appreciate its lovely, subtle smell. We can eat it and taste the nuanced flavors unique to the strawberry. We can digest it and fully benefit from its nutritional qualities. We can prepare it in a variety of delicious recipes. We can make paintings of it, write poems and sing songs about it (Strawberry Fields Forever), etc., etc.

So, let me ask you again, why do strawberries exist? What is the highest purpose for the existence of the strawberry? Is it not plainly obvious that it is here for US? Yes, the highest purpose of the simple yet wonderful strawberry is to be enjoyed and appreciated by human beings. Because we are the only creatures with the ability to FULLY appreciate the simple strawberry.

If it appears obvious that the strawberry exists for us, then what about the broader creation? Why do you think there exists breathtaking scenery in this world? If it were not for us, how could it be fully witnessed and appreciated? What about the abundant natural resources. Why are they there if not to be used by us to make and produce all the things from them that we dare to imagine.

Animals cannot fully appreciate or fully utilize this creation. I have never seen a dog paint a Mona Lisa. I have never heard of an armadillo composing a beautiful symphony. In all of time we have never seen a monkey design a two-story bungalow, build a steel framed bridge, invent a light bulb. Or for that matter learn to dance the tango, compose a touching poem, or sing a love song.

Not only are human beings perfectly equipped to fully appreciate and utilize all that this world provides, but we also possess the capability to elevate these very things. Yes, we elevate creation not only by our ability to fully make use of it, but also by our ability to consider, appreciate, and speak of it.

Is this not sufficient and obvious proof that this is why all things exist.... for US!!! What is the alternative? We would just have to chalk it up to a "super incredible coincidence" that these things "just happen" to be so. But no, because "coincidence" just like "chance" are myths. They are "no things". They have no power and therefore cannot cause anything. They are meaningless labels we use when we cannot understand or explain why things happen. So, we say "coincidence" or "chance" (more on this in a later chapter).

Is it not evidently obvious that all things are purposed? This is the all too obvious conclusion as to why things are. They have purpose and therefore, significance. The ultimate purpose and significance for all that exists in our world is for US to UTILIZE, APPRECIATE, AND ENJOY them. Because we are the ONLY ones best equipped to do this most fully. Animals and other life forms simply cannot.

This must mean that YOU are special, YOU are significant, YOU are IMPORTANT. This world was made FOR YOU!!!! If we fail to miss this overwhelmingly obvious conclusion, then shame on us.

Why does a car exist? Obviously, to be driven by human beings. Why does a radio exist? Obviously, so it can be listened to by humans. Everything in our man-made creation is purposed. The same must be deducted about our broader creation. We are specifically designed for this life and this life is specifically designed for US.

This fact is so very obvious that we would be foolish and blind to ignore it. Yet somehow, we have been hoodwinked into believing quite the opposite. We miss the most obvious conclusion and replace it with the fairy tale that we are merely accidents. That it is just by "chance" that we happen to occupy this privileged space in the universe.

However, if we can, for a minute, resist to subscribe to this simplistic, baseless, and ungrateful paradigm, then we can then begin to consider that maybe the most obvious conclusion is most true.

That we are not strangers in this life. Out of place, ill suited. But that we are perfectly equipped for this perfectly equipped world that was ready made for US. I know this may be hard for you to accept since we have been continually brainwashed with the opposite perspective. But, why not accept what seems plainly obvious? The conclusion that does not need any further scientific or other explanation. The conclusion that appears most obvious and that we are all qualified to accept, if we choose to.

"Life is not happening to you; life is happening for you"
Anthony Robbins

If we miss acknowledging this highest purpose of creation we under appreciate creation itself and in the process sell ourselves way short. We fail to rightly understand the proper context for our existence and the existence of all that surrounds us. When you accept this humbling, empowering, and most obvious truth, that the universe is here for us and we are perfectly equipped for it, then you have rightly set the stage for how you are to live. With a higher degree of purpose. That you were meant to live a life of confidence, victory, and of creative achievement.

Let me share a powerful perspective with you that you may not have considered before.

The Universe exists for US.
We do not exist for the Universe.

This realization struck me one day as I was sitting with my family in a Planetarium watching a presentation about the cosmos narrated by a popular comedian/actor. Maybe it was that very juxtaposition of listening to a serious presentation about the cosmos narrated by a comedian that helped me to see beyond the popular paradigm that was being perpetuated in her scripted narration.

This familiar paradigm that since the cosmos are so incredibly vast in comparison to us, that the logical conclusion must be that we are inconsequential and, thus, utterly insignificant. That we are sheer nothingness in comparison to all the "bigness" that is "out there". That we are nothing more than a fortunate coincidence. Merely a happy accident on the stage of this vast universe.

The tired and unprovable assumption that when we consider the vast expanse of the Cosmos the logical conclusion must be to automatically deduce that simply because of its 'bigness" and our comparable "smallness" that we must therefore be insignificant. A mere inconsequential spec of biological matter of little or no importance. Here today and gone tomorrow.

However, it was right there at that very moment, listening to this presentation, that it occurred to me in a total flash of un-influenced understanding and inspired awareness. What if the total opposite is true? What if the sheer vastness of the cosmos and the fact that, as far we can see, we are the only significant, intelligent beings in this ENTIRE physical universe is supposed to point us to a totally different conclusion? That we are not insignificant at all, but maybe, that we are MOST SIGNIFICANT. We are, after all, the only ones that can bear witness to the existence and majesty of these very cosmos. What if this points us to a totally different conclusion?

What if, precisely because we can observe and admire this vast expanse of marvelous space, positions us as the most privileged of observers. That is too obvious is it not? As far as we know, we are the ONLY ones that can appreciate this marvelous creation. We have a front row, VIP section seat to this show of shows.

What if the sheer breathtaking vastness of the observable universe is only meaningful and consequential precisely because we exist. What if it hangs out there for the single purpose of us bearing witness to it?

Devoid of our observation and appreciation of the universe it can be said that there is really nothing at all out there. Nothing really exists if there is no observer to acknowledge, assess, admire and ascribe meaning. Yes, what if the vastness of the marvelous cosmos that hangs there in infinity is intended precisely for us? To seek to understand it. To laud it, wonder, and marvel at it. Who else, or what else can do this but US? And if this is true then we are most SIGNIFICANT…we are, the KEY INGREDIENT.

This goes back to the age-old conundrum that asks: If a tree falls in the forest and there is no one there, does it make a sound? The answer is NO, it does not. Because for there to be a sound there must be an ear. And for there to be an ear, there must be a creature possessing that organ that has the ability to hear. Or a man-made device that has the ability to "hear" sound. Without the instrument of an ear there is no sound. There may be sound waves and vibrations and a disruption in the air pressure due to the physics of a falling tree. But there is NO sound without a "hearer". There is no reality without an observer. What would be the point?

Listen, I say we are NOT an accident. We are, in fact, the KEY ingredient. We are the consciousness that makes this all work. Would you make a high performing, luxury sports car if there were no one to drive it? Would you design a complex machine if it were not to be utilized by a capable and willing user? Would you compose a beautiful play if there was no audience?

What if the vast universe that surrounds and engulfs us is not evidence of our insignificance, but in fact obvious proof of our significance and privileged position in this creation?

I understand that there are those who will disagree with this position. Those who will continue to argue the opposite point. They would say that all the evidence points to our insignificance. Simply by the argument of equating size to significance. Which is not much of an argument. But if we are honest and objective I think we can agree that the evidence for that position is no more valid than the evidence for the opposing perspective.

So, if it simply comes down to a choice, of how YOU choose to process the available objective evidence to determine your conclusion, what would you choose?

Why deny yourself this? To believe that we are the privileged observes for which all this was created is not an empty boast or a statement of pride. To the contrary, it is to rightly assign even more worth and appreciation to all that is and has been created, because we now see it as being here for us. We therefore have a solemn duty to ascribe more value and worth to it. To appreciate and utilize it with a higher sense of responsibility and purpose. We are not dismissive and flippant by thinking "well, maybe all this just happens to be some sort of cosmic accident. So, what is the point?"

Listen, we would never ascribe a beautiful painting as the result of an explosion in a paint factory. Or a Maserati as the result of an explosion in an auto parts store. You get my point. So why would we be so intellectually dishonest by accepting this notion that there was a random explosion in the universe that produced the amazing order and purposeful design that we witness every day. We cannot and should not miss the obvious significance of PURPOSE. What is the purpose?

Everywhere we look we witness not just incredible beauty and complex systems of every kind. But more than that we are witnessing PURPOSE. If the purpose of this wonderful universe is to be here for US. What then is YOUR purpose? I say it is to live a life of gratitude and intentionality. To understand that we have been equipped with all the capabilities and resources we need to live empowered and productive lives.

In this book you will find truths that will enable you to realize your best self, Your Empowered Self. You are designed and perfectly suited to live and to thrive in this "made for you" universe. To live a life of gratitude and purposed accomplishment. I choose to believe in your significance, worth, and amazing capability. What about you?

Let us step forward together on the journey of empowerment in the pages that follow……

Empowerment Rule #1

Only You Stand In the Way of You

"The fault, dear Brutus, is not in our stars, but in ourselves"
Shakespeare

This is the foundational Empowerment rule that establishes the starting point on the journey towards realizing your Empowered Self. You cannot take step one on this journey until you embrace the profound truth that you are the only thing that stands in your way. That it is only ever you that can prevent you from becoming, achieving, or experiencing more in this life. Period.

Until you look in the mirror and take full responsibility for your attitudes, choices, actions, and yes, your circumstances, you will not experience the empowered life you are meant to live.

Over time we have accumulated a long and growing list of reasons why we are not happier, more fulfilled, more successful, etc. We have become experts at finding excuses and convenient rationalizations for our faults and shortcomings. We are quick to point an accusing finger at all the people, circumstances, and things we believe stand in our way.

We are prone to quickly label ourselves as victims of circumstance. Falsely believe that the issues, faults, and obstacles lie outside of us. In this state of self-delusion, we conveniently point to all the injustices, unfair situations, and problematic people in our lives. We complain that we can never catch a break, that unfortunate things always seem to happen to us, and that the odds are continually stacked against us.

We tend to fall into the "poor pitiful me" mode. Wrongly believing that seeking pity rather than taking full responsibility is the proper way to live. Secretly hoping that others will accept our mediocrity, forgive us our failings, or lower the expectations so we do not disappoint. And if we are lucky, maybe even get a handout.

We have become convinced that it is the outside situations and other people that victimize us. Sadly, these easy excuses and rationalizations have provided the feathering that makes us cozy and comfortable in our own nest of mediocrity and discontent.

But it is only when you embrace the truth that it has only ever been you getting in the way of you, that you can avail yourself of the power you rightly possess. The power to effect intentional change and positive outcomes in your life.

"No man is hindered by another.
He is only hindered by himself.
No man suffers because of another,
he suffers only because of himself"
James Allen

If you ignore this reality, you will continue to wrongly believe that you are the victim. Therefore, your empowerment will never be on display, and your life will never change. You must stop looking outward for your excuses and instead start looking inward. Accepting responsibility and thus, summoning your power.

To become empowered, you must take full responsibility and accept that there is no one, or no thing standing in your way. It is not your job, boss, wife, kids, the government, your parents, the economy, lack of good luck, your upbringing, etc....None of these things are what truly prevent you from achieving the better things you desire or long for. The truth is that the only thing standing in your way is YOU!!!

The journey towards Empowerment is marked by continual introspection. As you must always be willing to look within. Because it is only when you are truly honest and accept full responsibility for your attitudes, actions, and outcomes that you have the power to change. Remember, the power we possess always lies within us, never outside of us.

By making excuses and rationalizations we effectively ignore and lay down this power that is rightly ours. Because when our hands are too busy pointing accusatory fingers, they ignore and neglect the important and necessary work that only we can do in order to improve and move forward in our own lives.

One of the basic survival mechanisms we all possess is our ability to deflect and to rationalize. To save face and protect our self-esteem. To place the blame outside of us every chance we get. Fearing that an honest assessment will force us to look in the mirror where we will find the true culprit. Where we discover that our biggest nemesis and most formidable foe has always been and will always be, ourselves.

However, you must understand that an honest assessment or critique does not indict or minimize you. On the contrary, as you expose your own faults and failings this positions you to be able to move forward and grow. To become more of what you can rightly become.

While rationalizing can be a form of self-preservation, it also binds us to sameness and prevents us from growing. From becoming more and achieving more. It is the very act of self-preservation that holds us in the state of inertia and inaction where no change is possible. Effectively holding us back and keeping us in our state of discontent and unfulfillment.

Here is an important realization; In every situation you experience there is something significant that is revealed about YOU. As all external circumstances ultimately serve the purpose of revealing more of your true self.

"Circumstances does not make the man,
it reveals him to himself"
James Allen

For instance; if you are angry about a situation, there is something about YOU that is causing you to feel angry in that situation. If there is something that frustrates you about a situation. This points back to you, as there is something about YOU that is causing you the frustration in that situation.

If you are truly honest you will find that in every situation there is something about YOU that is the real cause. Because you hold the key that points to what got you IN a situation as well as what will get you OUT of a situation. As such, you must always be honest and humble, so you can discover the key part that you play. Because the cause and the solutions always reside in YOU.

All life is simply you, experiencing yourself by way of all the people and situations you encounter. It is the continual flow of events and circumstances in your life that serve to reveal more of who you are by way of your attitudes, thoughts, words, actions etc. Therefore, your life is to be seen as a continual self-discovery that leads you to more awareness, growth, and personal achievement.

"An unexamined life is not worth living"
Socrates

Of course, through your experiences, interactions, observations, etc. you will also inevitably learn about other people and situations. But everything you experience in life is mostly an opportunity for you to know yourself better. And in getting to know yourself better you can better direct your intentions to effect change in your thoughts, emotions, attitudes and actions. And in so doing to become empowered to effect more positive, intentional outcomes in your life.

"Man know thyself,
then thou shall know the Universe and God"
Pythagoras

Empowered thinking starts with a solemn commitment to NEVER, EVER indulge in the following:

Making excuses
Finding fault
Placing blame

The empowered person is not an excuse maker, fault finder, or blame maker. As these are all very disempowering, negative, and pointless activities. The empowered you has NO interest indulging in these. Since they will only serve to keep you in a state of delusion, discontent, and disempowerment.

The truth is that you are 100% responsible for your lot in this life. And that you only ever get what you truly deserve. So, take 100% responsibility, because it is YOUR life.

"The day that you discover that you
are in charge of your life,
is the day you turn your life around"
Patricia Fripp

How to make Impossible, Possible

Here is an interesting word play that makes a profound point. Look at the words "Impossible" and "Possible". What stands in the way of transforming the word "Impossible" into the word "Possible"?

What stands in the way are the letters "I" and "M". Because once you remove the letters "I" and "M" from the word "Impossible" you now have the word "possible". So, the answer is, that "IM" is what stands in the way of making impossible, possible.

This is much more than just an interesting word play. This is 100% true. Say it with me, "I'M the only thing that prevents me from making the impossible, possible in my life." Yes, the simple unavoidable truth is that it will only ever be YOU that stands in the way of you.

"Man is made or unmade by himself.
In the armory of thought he forges
the weapons by which he destroys himself.
He also fashions the tools with which
he builds for himself heavenly mansions
of joy and strength and peace"
James Allen

Your empowerment journey can only begin when you take full ownership for all the choices, attitudes, actions, and outcomes in your life. Accept and embrace this foundational first rule and you will start moving towards realizing a more empowered YOU.

I am confident that this truth will become increasingly clearer as we make our way through the pages of this book. So, strap yourself in for the Empowerment ride. The next two Empowerment Rules flow from this first and most foundational Rule. Enjoy!!

Empowerment Rule #2

If You Want Things To Change YOU Have To Change

"Be the change you want to see in the world"
Ghandi

If you want something or someone to change, you must change. This is such a simple, lovely, and refreshing rule. It reminds us that all we ever need to focus on, is simply on changing ourselves. Because when WE change, the entire world around us inevitably changes. And by us changing we can thus inspire and influence others to change. This is a powerful and EMPOWERING truth.

"When you change the way you look at things, the things you look at change"

But you may say "No, why do I need to change? I am not the problem, the problem is; my unrealistic boss, my demanding wife, my unappreciative kids, my needy dog, my hard-headed parents, etc.

They are the ones that need to change because they are the ones with issues, not I. They are the ones with the problem, or the ones causing the problem. It is not me, it is them.

NO, they are NOT the ones with the problem. YOU have the problem. Say it with me…If I want something or someone to change, I must change. I…. MUST…. CHANGE!!!!

This may be a frustrating realization at first, and it may not be what you want to hear. But, it is true and, guess what? Once embraced, it is truly EMPOWERING.

Listen, you only have the power to change YOU. You do not have the power to force other people to change. Other people and situations will only change once YOU have changed. And yes, you do have the power to change your own attitudes, expectations, judgements, choices, actions, etc.

The reason why other people change when you change is because we are relational beings. We do not operate in a vacuum. We are continually influencing, reacting, and responding to one another. Always initiating and receiving feedback and input from one another. We are all very influential, and at the same time very prone to being influenced. We exert tremendous influence over each other, both consciously and subconsciously.

Let me give you a very simple example that illustrates how much influence we have over one another. Have you ever been in the same room with someone and they start to sing or hum a song? Then, without you realizing it, you also start to sing that song, either in your head or maybe even out loud. Often you may not even be aware that you are singing that particular song or that it got "stuck" in your head because your friend, spouse, or coworker started singing it first. It just happened unconsciously because of the power of suggestion and influence.

I know this is a simple example, but it does provide proof of how susceptible we all are to being influenced. We influence and are influenced by one another in very powerful and profound ways. Beyond what we will ever fully realize.

Think of someone who has influenced you in this life. How about something that someone said to you that has always stayed with you? An encouraging or complimentary word that you have always treasured. Or maybe someone once said something hurtful to you that you have never forgotten and still carry with you as a scar.

We influence one another in deep ways. Why is it that it is often said "be careful of the company you keep"? Well, it's because they have the power to influence you. So, you should be careful who you surround yourself with. Jim Rohn said that we become the average of the five people we spend most of our time with. This is because of the power of influence. We are continually influencing and being influenced by others.

"If you hang out with chickens you are going to cluck, and if you hang out with eagles you are going to fly."
Dr. Steve Maraboli

Let me share a personal example of a time when I applied this empowerment rule of changing myself to change a situation. I have a teenage daughter, and I have learned that interesting things happen when children turn into teenagers. One of the strange phenomenon I have experienced is that when children become teenagers, Dad suddenly becomes invisible. When they are young, your children can't seem to get enough of you. They're always wanting to be with you to play a game, read a book, just talk, etc. When you come home from work they excitedly come running to greet you. Insisting to be picked up and carried. You feel important and appreciated by them. You are their favorite person. But, when they become teenagers, Dad suddenly and inexplicably becomes… invisible.

I could be in any room of the house and my teen age daughter would pass by without even the slightest indication that she was aware of my presence. Even if I had been away on business for days. When I would come home she still seemed totally ignorant of the fact that I exist.

In this situation it is easy for a parent to feel unappreciated, disrespected, hurt, angry, sad, etc. A father cannot help but think, "How dare she ignore me like that? She does not even say good morning, goodbye, or how are you Dad?" "Doesn't she realize that I am the one that provides for her. I buy her all the things she needs and wants; her clothes, her new cell phone, etc. How dare she act this way? What an ungrateful and inconsiderate child" And on, and, on and on. It is easy for a parent to feel like the victim in this situation.

But, now I know better. I know that if I want something or someone to change, I must change. I no longer burden the other person with the need to change. I realize that it is for ME to take the initiative and change myself. Change my attitude, emotion, judgements, expectations, actions, etc. This is the only logical and empowering realization.

The instant I embraced that truth, my attitude immediately changed. I was now willing to reach out to my daughter in a more loving, patient, and understanding way. Rather than becoming angry, resentful, or having negative feelings towards her. I was no longer judgmental of her, which was only serving to further damage our relationship. Instead, I focused on my emotions and my actions. I took charge of me.

My changing is powerful because it "fixes" me right away. But there is another interesting side effect. The other person also starts to change. Why do they change? Well, because since I have changed, and they are being affected by and responding to my actions and attitudes, they will also, inevitably, change.

"Our life is what our thoughts make it.
A man will find that as he alters
his thoughts towards things and other people,
things and other people will alter towards him"
James Allen

You see, if you expect someone to change in order to accommodate your expectations, it may never happen. Or, it may take a long time for it to happen. You don't have the time to wait, because during that time (if it ever does come) the relationship suffers and will deteriorate. Becoming less than what it could be. This empowerment rule is especially important in the effect it can have on our intimate relationships. But this applies to all relationships.

When I change, whether it is my attitude, approach, expectations, judgements, prejudices, etc. There is an IMMEDIATE change in ME. In MY feelings, emotions, and yes, in my reality. In this specific example with my teenage daughter, I experienced an immediate positive change in the quality of my relationship with her the minute I realized that I was the one that needed to change.

I could give you many more examples of this simple EMPOWERING rule. But I am sure that if you think about it, you also will find examples in your own life that proves this rule to be true. When you change, everything else changes including the people around you. Because they cannot help but react differently to the now different you.

Realize that any change you want to see must start with you, and you will be immediately liberated to start more positively impacting your relationships and situations.

"Change your conception of yourself
and you will automatically change
the world in which you live.
Do not try to change people;
they are only messengers telling you who you are.
Revalue yourself and they will confirm the change"
Neville Goddard

Once your attitudes, emotions, and actions in any situation changes, it is no longer even necessary for the situation or the other person to change. Since it no longer presents a problem for you. You now see it as an opportunity for learning, a challenge to overcome, a lesson to make you wiser, a test to make you stronger, etc.…You are immediately in a more EMPOWERED state of being. You are no longer feeling victimized or wronged by the other person or situation. You are in control when you realize that what is needed is for you to change your attitude, expectations, perspective, emotions, actions, etc.

If you want something or someone to change, YOU must change. Use this rule in your relationships and you will enjoy much more rewarding, happy, fulfilling relations.

"Your life does not get better by chance,
it gets better by change"
Jim Rohn

The three EMPOWERMENT HABITS that follow provide insights and suggestions on ways in which you can change and improve. Embracing these habits will empower you to more positively impact all of your relationships.

Empowerment Habit:

Be Kind

"Everyone you meet is fighting a battle you know nothing about. Be kind. Always."
Wendy Mass

I AM…. Kind. I have deep respect and appreciation for all people. Because I believe they are worthy and deserving of my kindness and love.

To properly and consistently apply this empowerment habit you must embrace a mindset that says: "Treat others BETTER than you expect to be treated." This should be your attitude when dealing with people in any and every situation. As it sets the highest standard for acting in the most selfless, kind, and loving manner.

Every Human Being Has Intrinsic Value

You think you a special, right? Of course, you do. You love yourself. You take care of yourself, feed yourself, bathe yourself, dress yourself, etc. You take care of yourself because you are all you have. You love yourself as you should, since you are the most important person to you.

Well, others feel the same way about themselves as you do about you. Of course, we all differ to the degree of self-love, self-worth etc.…but these are just degrees of the same inclination we all share. The fundamental inclination of self-love and preservation. This is not selfish, but necessary and practical. So, understanding this, it follows that we should acknowledge and respect others. We must be kind, gracious, considerate, sensitive, encouraging, and loving to one another.

"Love your neighbor as yourself"
Mark 12:31

We must always demonstrate a loving attitude towards all people, because in doing so we rightly acknowledge and honor the inherent dignity and worth that, just like you, every other person is also endowed with.

You must have this belief as a core foundation; that every human being is worthy and deserving of your love and kindness. Because they are image bearers of the divine. We all possess that spark of the creator that ignites our individual worthiness. Therefore, love should be the hallmark of our inclination towards one another.

"If a man looks upon any other man
and estimates that man as less than himself,
then he is stealing from the other.
He is stealing the other's birthright-that of equality"
Neville Goddard

Embracing and living this attitude empowers you to become a more uplifting and gracious person. And, as you treat others with kindness and love you will encourage and empower them in the process.

What is Love?

We tend to mistakenly identify love as an emotion. As some sort of fuzzy feeling that can be both, incredibly strong, yet also fickle and fleeting. Here today and gone tomorrow. We see the effect of this is in relationships all the time. Husband and wife come together in "love" but then the relationship falls apart and that same love that once brought them together fades and is "no longer there".

This begs the question. Is love a fickle butterfly that gingerly dances on this flower then the next? Beautiful, wonderful, all consuming, but fleeting? And if spooked, for any reason, will flitter away when least expected? Is love incapable of maintaining an enduring relationship? Is it not the glue that holds all things together? How are we to more rightly understand this thing called love? How can we more accurately define, know, and experience it? If it is in fact the glue that holds all things together then we must get to know Love better.

The most complete and correct definition of Love is found in the classic Bible chapter, 1 Corinthians 13. Where love is defined in this way:

Love is patient, love is kind,
it does not envy or boast.
It is not arrogant or rude.
It does not insist on its own way.
It is not imposing, it is not proud,
it is not self-seeking.
It is not easily angered,
it keeps no record of wrongs.
It does not delight in wrongdoing
but rejoices with the truth.
It always protects, always trusts,
always hopes, always perseveres.
Love never fails.
Love is the most excellent way.

Think about this most "lovely" definition. It teaches us that there is no love if it is not demonstrated by loving actions. Because love can only be love when it is intentionally demonstrated in our words, attitudes, and actions. A love that is not continually bearing fruit by way of corresponding and continual loving attitudes and actions is no love at all.

Read this definition over and over. Know it, embrace it and live it. As this is LOVE. Any other definition is fakery and does not rightly define true Love. Love is more rightly understood, not as an emotion, but as an intentional choice to act and respond in ways that qualify as loving. Always remember, LOVE is a verb.

Love, a Powerful Binding Agent

Love is the most powerful binding agent in our human experience. In chemistry we are taught that there is a force that binds the basic elements together. These strong bonds are the glue that hold together the materials that furnish all physical existence. These atomic bonds are more powerful than anything we know of. And when they are controlled and unleashed, we can create atomic explosions that can devastate and cause unthinkable destructive outcomes.

Think about love the same way. It is the glue that binds all human interactions and relations together. To the degree that there is love there is peace, harmony, and good. All things are bound together. However, if this force is taken out, is out of balance, or not strong enough. Then what results is devastation and loss.

Where there is lack of love, relationships disintegrate, families are splintered, and societies lose their light. Without love what we are left with is hate, envy, frustration, selfish pride, etc. And these are all destructive emotions that lead to catastrophic negative outcomes.

To the degree that there is love (demonstrated by loving actions) then there exists a powerful and effective bonding agent in that relationship. The relationship is therefore less likely to become fragmented, diminished, or pulled apart. Because of the continual loving actions that bind it together. It is in displaying loving actions that love is active and becomes the effective glue that can powerfully bind relationships together.

To the extent that love is absent there is no binding agent, only superficial emotions or temporary lust. Relationships can exist for the moment while the superficial emotions are present. But these emotions are, at best, fickle and fleeting. They have no long-lasting power to hold relationships together.

The only true force that can keep relationships whole, strong, and long lasting is Love. A Love that is patient and kind. Not envious or boastful. Not arrogant or rude. Not insistent on its own way. Not imposing, proud, or self-seeking. Not easily angered. Not consumed with keeping record of wrongs. A love that is always protecting, always trusting, always hoping, always persevering. This is the love that never fails. This is the love that is truly the most excellent way. And this is the love that is binding and lasting.

"All you need is Love,
Love is all you need"
John Lennon/Paul McCartney

We are to continually demonstrate love towards one another. It is more than a platitude, it is a duty. We have a continuing debt that we owe to one another. And this is to love one another. When we fail to act in love, we have in fact, incurred a very real debt. And to settle the debt, we must ask for forgiveness.

Empowerment Habit:

Be Forgiving

"Forgiveness is the fragrance that the violet sheds on the heel that has crushed it"
Mark Twain

I AM…Forgiving. I know that if I do not forgive, I have simply placed on my shoulders a heavy burden. Therefore, I am always quick to forgive and forget. I live and let live.

Be quick to forgive. And to continue forgiving. Do not hold resentments. Because when you hold grudges, they become poison to your soul. They sour your disposition and rob you of your joy. Grudges are very heavy burdens. When we forgive, we free ourselves from that burden. It takes work to stay angry. It can be both physically, emotionally, and mentally taxing.

"To be angry is to revenge the fault of others on ourselves"
Alexander Pope

Sadly, we often feel like it is our duty to stay angry or to hold a grudge. We feel that in some cases it is appropriate and even mandatory that we should stay mad or hold on to negative feelings about others. Because of something they did, or something they said to us, or about us.

We wrongly believe that staying angry or holding a grudge will serve some sort of irrational justice that is our duty to dispense. We are deceived into believing that it would not be right if we did not hold on to a grudge. Sadly, we keep the hurt alive within us. Allowing this poison of negativity and ill will to continually afflict us in the process.

We are not to live by the barbaric adage of "an eye for an eye". It is not our place to seek retribution. Leave justice and retribution to God. As He is the ultimate judge, not you. We are not qualified or authorized to be the dispensers of justice and retribution. This is not our duty. We are to forgive and forget. When we forgive we also benefit because we have laid down a heavy burden.

"To err is human; to forgive, divine."
Alexander Pope

Trust in Positive Intentions

A very important element of being kind and cultivating positive relations is to always trust in positive intentions. Resist the natural inclination to automatically jump to conclusions or make negative assumptions about other people's intentions.

Assuming that others have negative intentions toward you will surely undermine your relationships. Because indulging this attitude will set you on a negative edge. It will cause you to project adversarial, antagonistic attitudes. This will result in negative actions which will only serve to diminish and bring decay to any relationship.

Always give people the benefit of the doubt. Trust that they have their own, just reasons for doing the things they do, or for saying the things they say. To always assume that others have negative intentions towards you or are "out to get you" is a sure way to poison any relationship and eventually destroy it.

First, we are NOT qualified to assume what other people's true intentions are. Because we simply just don't know, so we should leave it at that. Allow others the courtesy to be who they are and do what they do.

Secondly, why would you automatically jump to assume the worst of all possible intentions? This is negative and results in negative outcomes. We become troubled and hurt by this type of thinking. It only results in self-inflicted wounds.

Do not burden yourself or others with this negative heavy lifting. I suggest that you not indulge in making ANY negative assumptions at all about other people's intentions. It is far better to assume that they have only positive intentions in mind and that we just tend to misunderstand, misjudge, or misread them.

"Never ascribe to malice what can be rightly explained by incompetence"

I would also add to this last quote that many times other people's "incompetence" may stem from their ignorance, insensitivity, or indifference, etc. Regardless, we should still refrain from ascribing their actions or intents to malice.

Assuming people have negative intentions is a sure way to undermine relationships and cause conflict and grief. Also, to assume that we rightly know other people's intentions is simply arrogant and presumptive.

Give others the benefit of the doubt. Remember that they too are struggling to get by in this life, they also have their share of burdens, doubts, insecurities and fears. As you trust in positive intentions this will pre-dispose you to having more positive and empowered relations and interactions.

Empowerment Habit:

Be Well Spoken

"Be careful with your words, once they are said, they can only be forgiven, not forgotten"
Unknown

I AM…Well Spoken. I speak positive, encouraging, empowering words. Words that heal, comfort, strengthen, and inspire. Words that always serve to build up, never to tear down.

Words are your first level of creation into the physical world. Your thoughts and ideas you can keep to yourself. Your emotions are a bit harder to contain. But, once you speak, it is out there. You have now created something for the world to hear and be impacted by.

Ask yourself, "what do I sound like?" I don't mean your volume, tone, or inflection (while these are important). I mean what words are you putting out there? What messages are you continually broadcasting? What is the predominant content and tone of your communications? What are you creating with your words? What thoughts, ideas, attitudes, or mental images are you literally breathing to life by way of your words?

"Your words can calm the angry, uplift the despondent, goad the quitter, cheer the unhappy, warm the lonely, praise the worthy, encourage the defeated, teach the ignorant"
Og Mandino

Are you speaking positively, or are you a source of negativity, complaining, fault finding, excuse making? Are you building up, or tearing down? Your words have the power to hurt or heal; embitter or enlighten; discourage or empower.

"There is one whose words are like sword thrusts, but the tongue of the wise brings healing"
Proverbs 12:18

The empowered person is mindful of their words because they know that there is great power in them. Additionally, they understand that the first recipient of your own words is YOU. So, are they negative and discouraging, or positive and empowering?

Your words can be a lovely fragrance that can permeate and uplift any situation. Or, they can be like gasoline, carelessly and recklessly poured onto a raging fire.

Think about something someone has said to you, or about you, that hurt or offended you. Conversely, think about something positive that someone has said to you, or about you, that encouraged and uplifted you. One is negative and hurt you deeply, while the other is a lovely gem that always brings you joy and confidence.

People's lives can literally be turned around in a positive or negative way by the words that are spoken to them. Knowing this, you must be gracious, kind, and complimentary with your words. You must speak light and hope. Make the conscious decision to always be gracious, positive, and uplifting with your speech.

We are all on this journey of life together. And we all know that at times life can be challenging and burdensome. Therefore, we should always seek to lift each other up, not tear each other down.

The words we project and the words we hear from others will, to some degree, echo within us our entire lives. As the subconscious mind keeps a perfect record of all the sensory input we receive. We all carry within us the memory of all things that have been said to us, whether hurtful or encouraging.

Sadly, because of our insecurity and pride, we are often prone to spout words that are less than considerate or kind. This is an ever-present temptation that we must always seek to resist and re-direct. Consider that the tongue is a powerful weapon and you should therefore be very careful to wield it with discernment and positive intentions. Resist speaking careless, insensitive, or hurtful words. Being careless or reckless with your words can cause severe harm to ourselves and others.

"Be sure to taste your words before you spit them out"

Wrongly thinking that our words have no real consequence, it is far too easy to speak in careless, insensitive ways, or to be reckless with our words. Because, after all, they are "just words". But, the fact of the matter is that our words have a tremendous impact not only in the moment, but beyond. Our words are an awesome force that we should always use for the good.

The saying "Sticks and stones will break my bones, but words will never hurt me" is not true. Because no matter how much we pretend that we are not hurt by what other people say to us or about us. The truth is, that to some extent, we cannot avoid feeling hurt by negative, accusatory, unkind, insensitive, or mean-spirited words.

Negative and unkind words always serve to tear away a little bit of the person they are directed towards. Hurtful words seep into our soul no matter how much we try to protect ourselves by pretending they do not matter, or that they don't hurt.

Always have a kind word for all. Resist and avoid speaking negatively or judgmentally of others in order to make yourself feel more important, or better than others. Do not be deceived. You are only as big as you are. No more and no less. Attempting to make others seem small only takes you down in size with them. Always take the high road, the view is far better from there.

Do not allow others to drag you into negative, disempowering conversations that are filled with gossip, back stabbing, or are disparaging towards others. We should not indulge in this as it only results in negative emotions and outcomes. Be a light in your circle of conversations. If you feel a conversation is getting negative, gossipy, or unkind, simply stop and change the subject. This will have a positive impact as most people are not conscious of how negative conversations create a cloud of disempowered baggage that now gets carried around by all.

Sadly, most people have developed poor habits in this area. They simply cannot help themselves when it comes to speaking negatively or judgmentally of others. It is too easy and too tempting. However, as for you, do not indulge it. Do them a favor, call it out respectfully and kindly. Tactfully say something like, "I am not comfortable where this conversation is going, can we change the subject.?" Or, "how about we talk about something more positive" etc.

"Without wood a fire goes out;
without a gossip a quarrel dies down"
Proverbs 26:20

Avoid Argumentation

Are you quick to get into arguments? Arguing is a form of negative and disempowering speaking. Remember that it takes two to argue. It is impossible for an argument to happen if one person refuses to participate. It is a bit like clapping. Unless both hands are involved there is no clapping.

Avoid the trap of falling into arguments. It is a wonderful skill to be able to navigate any conversation clear of argumentation. Be agreeable and understanding. Always accepting and acknowledging the other persons viewpoint. Do not feel like you have to defend yourself continually.

One way to avoid arguments is to always remind yourself that others have the right to choose their own views, beliefs, attitudes, and responses. Whether we agree or disagree with someone else's position or point of view, we must always respect their right to having them. Even though you may totally disagree with a particular position or opinion. It is still your duty to respect the other person's right to their own opinion.

The reason why we must always respect others opinions is because, just like you have a right to your opinions and beliefs, others also have that same right to hold ANY view they desire. Honor this right and you will find yourself much less apt to fall into heated arguments or disagreements.

"A gentle answer turns away wrath,
but a harsh word stirs up anger"
Proverbs 15:1

It is not your job to win people over to your way of thinking, but it is always your duty to show respect and to allow others their right to be or think whatever they choose. Plus, you will also be less inclined to become emotional when trying to convince others of your deeply held views or beliefs. If you can sway others to your side, great, but this is not your role in the world.

"The modest way in which I proposed my opinion procured them a readier reception and less contradiction"
Ben Franklin

At the end of the conversation it is far better to leave as friends rather than enemies. Always remember that we are all fighting the same fight. We all face our own daily struggles, challenges, fears, and frustrations in this life. So, treat others with more kindness. Allowing other people to hold wrong positions is a form of respect and kindness. I may disagree with you, but I still respect you. If I cannot convince you, what do I gain if I then also make you my enemy or alienate you in the process? Live and let live. Your burden will be lighter.

A practical tip to avoid getting into negative arguments is to use the word "I" rather than "you" when you are in a disagreement or conflict. Speaking in terms of how "I" feel about something, or why "I" believe a certain thing. Is a far better approach than attacking the other person's views or beliefs by using the word "YOU".

For instance, instead of saying "you always do that" in an accusatory manner. You can instead say, "I feel hurt when you do that". This is a far more effective and more positive way to get your point across.

It is always far safer, and more honest to speak in terms of "I" as you can always rightly and honestly speak on your own behalf. However, when using the word "you" we will be perceived in an accusatory or judgmental manner. When we do, we intrude on the right of the other person to be who they are and to choose their actions and behaviors.

Speak of your negative emotions. Don't act on them

Another very practical and positive habit is to speak of your negative emotions, rather than show them. We are emotional beings and cannot avoid experiencing negative emotions at times. But we know all too well that when we act out of our negative emotions only negative outcomes follow. So, it is wiser to speak of your negative emotions rather than show them. It is far better to say things like; "I feel very angry right now" or "What you did really frustrated me", "I am very upset at this time" etc. Rather than to act out those emotions in your words, tone, or actions. It is much more positive and productive to calmly and kindly say that you are upset, disappointed, angry, hurt, etc. rather than acting or speaking out of those destructive emotions.

When we act out of those negative emotions it will surely add fuel to an already fiery situation and no one will win. As the fire will inevitably burn both participants. Acting out of negative emotions will only ever produce more negative responses and outcomes.

Speak Decisively and Confidently

When you speak about wanting or doing you must choose your words more carefully. You should not say "I am going to do this". Instead you should say; "I am doing this" as this choice of words already puts you in that decision and denotes commitment. It places you in that state of DOING, and not "going to do". There is NO "going to do" there should only be the state of doing or not doing. As this is the active and empowered state. You shouldn't say "I am going to get it", you should say "I am getting it". Always speak in the "right here, right now" mode. As this is more empowering.

If you decide you want to start getting up earlier, then reinforce this choice by saying I am **getting** up at 6am tomorrow". Rather than "I am **going** to get up at 6 am tomorrow". Say "I am losing 5 pounds in the next two weeks" rather than, "I am going to lose 5 lbs. in the next two weeks" etc....Speaking in the present reinforces your intention and already starts to manifest the reality of your decision.

Refuse to indulge in negative speak. Eliminate words like "can't, hate, bad, problem, frustrating, awful", etc..... In short, don't say the things that you do not want. Avoid negative phrases like "Can't seem to make this work". "I am terrible at this", "I can't stand when this happens", etc. Instead choose phrases like "I will make this happen", "I will get better at this" etc.

Never speak like a victim. Closely censor your vocabulary. Catch and correct yourself when you are using negative and disempowering words and phrases. Remember that you are never a victim unless you choose to be and as such you must NEVER speak like a victim. As this will only serve to disempower and drain you of your energy and positive intentionality.

Use the words that speak of what you desire. Pick words that always suit the occasion in a positive and empowering way. Words that everyone can receive and that will result in a positive response. Pick your words very carefully.

Avoid sarcasm, and exaggeration. As these are negative and are usually intended at making someone else feel inferior.

Remember that when you speak, you are not only directing your words to others. But, just as important, you are speaking to yourself. You are also part of the listening audience. So, as you speak with others you are not only impacting and influencing them, but you are also impacting and further influencing yourself. All the more reason to be mindful of your words and to always speak in the most positive and empowering ways.

Your speaking is a creative act. Make your speech lovely, kind, positive, and inspiring. Always encourage and build up others and yourself by your empowering choice of words.

***"If you want to change your life,
begin by changing your words.
Start speaking the words of your dreams,
of who you want to become,
not the words of fear and failure"***
Robert Kiyosaki

Empowerment Rule #3

<u>If You Want Things To Get Better YOU Have To Get Better</u>

"<u>Life does not get easier, you just get better</u>"

This empowerment rule begs for practical application. If you want things to get better, one certain way to make that happen, is for YOU to get better at that thing.

Do you want a relationship to get better?
YOU get better at relationships.

Do you want your love life to get better?
YOU become a better lover.

Do you want your sales number to increase?
YOU become a better salesperson.

Do you want to improve the profitability or efficiency of your company or team?
YOU get better at understanding and leading in this area. Etc.....

You see, there is nothing or no one preventing you from the better things, better results, or better experiences you desire. Once again, the finger points at YOU. You must look in the mirror where you find that. "Wherever you go, there you are." You cannot escape the effect of YOU. It is only ever YOU that is defining and limiting your capabilities, experiences, and outcomes. It has been you all along. Own it and move on. In a more positive, empowered direction.

Listen, we all hope, dream, and desire to experience better things. As this is a natural and normal inclination of all human beings. Who wouldn't want better things, relationships or results? Of course, we all do. Well, since we all long for better things then we should get a full and more complete understanding of this concept of "better".

The concept of "better" has subjective and objective elements. It is subjective in that it is relative, since it must be understood in relation and comparison to something that already is. For instance, let's say you own a brand-new Mercedes Benz and I own a motor scooter. And I now purchase a used Honda Civic, that would be better for me. But that would not be better for you, since you already own a brand-new Mercedes. Which is arguably a "better" car.

So, the idea of "better" in this case is subjective. Because it is dependent on the context, and the existing thing that is being considered or compared to. This is the subjective element of the concept of "better". A "better" something for me may not necessarily be "better" for you.

However, there is also the objective element of the concept of "better". And that is that "Better" will always mean, DIFFERENT. Because the better thing will ALWAYS be different than the existing thing. This is a subtle, but powerful way to understand the idea of "better". Better will always be.... Different

<u>Better = Different</u>

This Empowerment Rule says; If you want something to get better. YOU, must be better. But it is not until you realize that better really means different, that this truly hits home. Yes, if you want something better, or if you want to be better, you must be willing to be DIFFERENT. You must be willing to think, believe, expect, speak, feel, or act DIFFERENTLY. The empowerment lies in this realization that better will always mean DIFFERENT.

You must be willing to do things differently. Or do different things altogether. Because this is the ONLY way for you to realize the "better" thing or result you seek or desire. This is closely tied to the previous empowerment rule that states; If You Want Something to Change, You Have to Change.

This makes perfect sense, and more importantly it presents us with a very practical means by which we can seek to improve in EVERY area of life. Just seek to be different!! Think different, expect different, act different, speak different, etc.....

However, there is one major catch. We know that change is something we all tend to resist. So, this creates an interesting dilemma. In order to get what we most want, those better things or experiences, we must do what we most tend to resist? YES, that is exactly right.

To get the better things you want.
You have to do the thing that
you instinctively resist…
CHANGE!!!

Why is it that we so resist change? Why is it that most of us have this addiction to sameness? What is it on the other side of change that we fear? After all, isn't variety the spice of life? Isn't change the only constant in life?

The Power of Precedent

One reason we resist change is because of the power of precedent. Because once a precedent has been set, there is a strong tendency to follow in that path. Once an action or process is initiated, a precedent has been set and it carries with it the force of inertia. Once a path has been taken (in thought or action) that brings with it a form of gravity, automatically pulling us in that direction. No matter how crooked, uncomfortable, or unproductive a path may be, there will nonetheless be a natural tendency to follow it. For no other reason than it has already been marked out and brought forth. This is the power of precedent, and it is wonderfully illustrated in the poem below.

The Calf-Path
Sam Foss

One day through the primeval wood
A calf walked home as good calves should;
But made a trail all bent askew,
A crooked trail as all calves do.
Since then three hundred years have fled,
And I infer the calf is dead.
But still he left behind his trail,
And thereby hangs my moral tale.

The trail was taken up next day,
By a lone dog that passed that way;
And then a wise bell-wether sheep
Pursued the trail o'er vale and steep,
And drew the flock behind him, too,
As good bell-wethers always do.
And from that day, o'er hill and glade.
Through those old woods a path was made.

And many men wound in and out,
And dodged, and turned, and bent about,
And uttered words of righteous wrath,
Because 'twas such a crooked path;
But still they followed—do not laugh—
The first migrations of that calf,
And through this winding wood-way stalked
Because he wobbled when he walked.

This forest path became a lane,
that bent and turned and turned again;
This crooked lane became a road,
Where many a poor horse with his load
Toiled on beneath the burning sun,
And traveled some three miles in one.
And thus, a century and a half
They trod the footsteps of that calf.

The years passed on in swiftness fleet,
The road became a village street;
And this, before men were aware,
A city's crowded thoroughfare.
And soon the central street was this
Of a renowned metropolis;

And men two centuries and a half,
Trod in the footsteps of that calf.
Each day a hundred thousand rout
Followed the zigzag calf about
And o'er his crooked journey went
The traffic of a continent.

A Hundred thousand men were led,
By one calf near three centuries dead.
They followed still his crooked way,
And lost one hundred years a day;
For thus such reverence is lent,
To well established precedent.

A moral lesson this might teach
Were I ordained and called to preach;
For men are prone to go it blind
Along the calf-paths of the mind,
And work away from sun to sun,
To do what other men have done.
They follow in the beaten track,
And out and in, and forth and back,

And still their devious course pursue,
To keep the path that others do.
They keep the path a sacred groove,
Along which all their lives they move.
But how the wise old wood gods laugh,
Who saw the first primeval calf.
Ah, many things this tale might teach.
But I am not ordained to preach.

This insightful poem eloquently illustrates how the power of precedent is responsible for setting into motion much of our purposeless, mindless trotting. We must understand and accept that it is most often because of precedent that we build up immovable edifices of inefficiency in our lives. Simply because we are prone to being creatures of habit.

We often create winding paths of thoughts or actions for no other reason than because of precedent. We veer to the left at this point or that point, simply because we have always done so. For no reason other than it is what we may have done yesterday.

The Law of Inertia

Behind the power of precedent lies the law of inertia. Which is what gives precedent its effectiveness. The definition of inertia is: "A tendency to do nothing or to remain unchanged". The Physics definition is: "A property of matter by which it continues in its existing state of rest or uniform motion in a straight line, unless that state is changed by an external force.

Inertia is an unavoidable physical law. We are all subject to this universal force that not only affects our physical state, but our thinking and emotional states as well. It is continuously pulling on us. Causing us to stay in a state of "no change". Keeping us in our comfort zones.

The empowered individual must be able to see their comfort zone for what it truly is. It is the very state that holds us back from changing, from being different. From obtaining the better things we truly desire.

You will continue to be comfortable, in your "comfort zones" until you realize that the source of the real discomfort is your own unwillingness to move out of your "comfort zone". I know that sounds a bit confusing, so let me say it more simply. Your "comfort zone" is really your "discomfort zone". As it is your comfort zone that is the cause of your unwillingness to change and thus the true root cause of much of your discontent.

So, we must rename this concept of "Comfort Zone" and call it what it truly is, the "dis-comfort zone". Or more technically let's call it, the "INERTIA ZONE". Because, when you think about it, it is really you being held captive by inertia.

The effects of the law of inertia are unavoidable; however, not irresistible. It can be overcome. To overcome the force of inertia you simply need to apply a greater external or internal force that causes a change of direction or momentum.

In order to change, we must be continually applying a greater force in our lives. This force of change can only come from within. It may be influenced by outside elements but ultimately it is an inside force that has the power to move us in a different direction.

"Our desire to change must be greater than our desire to stay the same."

The prior quote is more accurately stated like this:
"Our desire to change must be greater than our **tendency** to stay the same." Because, you see, we don't really have a desire to stay the same. Our desire is for BETTER, which means different. But, it is our **tendency** to stay the same. We **tend** to stay the same. Not because we desire it, but because of the law of inertia having its effect over us. Holding us captive in our comfort, or familiar zones. Keeping us trotting along the familiar calf paths of our own making.

The effect of this law of sameness and inertia causes us to stay bound to our current ideas, thoughts, feelings, and routines. Guaranteeing that nothing will change.

When we will not change on the inside then no outside change can take place.

Since the reason you tend NOT to change is because you are comfortable in your "comfort zones". You must see your unwillingness to change as the real reason preventing you from realizing your true wants and desires. You must associate your state of inertia, your condition of "no change" as the "painful zone". Because it is the true source, and cause of your discontent.

The real reason for the deepest discontent in our lives is not because we do not have certain things, results, or relations. Our true discontent in life comes from the fact that deep, deep inside, if we are truly honest with ourselves, we know that we do not have these "better" things we long for because we are not willing to make the changes needed in order to get them.

Yes, if we are honest, we know we can get them, but we also know that to get them involves having to change. And we are not willing to pay that price, to make that change. To think different, to act different, to be different. So, the TRUE reason we are discontent is not because of our unfulfilled hopes, dreams, and desires. But because we are simply not willing to change in order to realize them. It is never that we can't, it is that we don't. We refuse to let go of our familiar mediocrity in order to embrace a new attitude or mindset. We don't have better because we are unwilling to change in order to get it.

"Men are anxious to improve their circumstances, but are unwilling to improve themselves, they therefore remain bound"
James Allen

It is our propensity to stay the same, to remain unchanged, that is the true cause of much of our discontent. Here again you are pointed back to Empowerment Rule #1. The only thing that stands in the way of you, is YOU.

As part of building your empowerment mentality you must view change as good, as necessary, as vital. Not only should you NOT resist change, but you should embrace it, and even, dare I say, pursue it. You must be on a willing journey of continual change. Acknowledging and embracing that each day the old you should bring forth a new you. Each new day is an opportunity for you to change and take a step closer to a better you. A more empowered you.

In order to realize that better "you" and move towards the better things you desire, you must apply a greater force that will continuously cause you to change and be different. This greater force that you possess lies in the **power of your intentions**. You must create strong intentional wants. You must WANT to change. You must WANT to do the things that will bring you those things you desire. The focus must be on the WANT. Because once you develop strong enough wants, then your WILL follows, enabling you to do what is necessary to realize what it is you desire.

Want vs Will

To become masterful at causing intentional changes in our lives it is important to better understand the relationship between our "want" and our "will". We must clarify between the things that we desire and the things that we ultimately do and realize.

You may think that your want and your will are one in the same, but they are not. They are distinct faculties that overlap and work very closely together.

Let's start by taking a closer look at the familiar paradigm that tells us that we have "will power". All our lives we have heard that we have this faculty called will power, and that we must apply it in order to make those difficult or challenging things happen in our lives.

We hear this type of language all the time. "Use your will power", "It takes will power". Or "I have no will power", etc. What is will power? The textbook definition sounds something like this: "The faculty by which a person decides on and initiates action" The ability to control oneself, strong determination that allows you to do something difficult"

You must re-construct this faulty paradigm. The truth is that your power does not really lie in your will, but in your wants. What you really have is **WANT POWER**. You must first, truly WANT something. Because when you want it bad enough then you WILL get it.

The will to do something must always be preceded by the want to do it. Because, ultimately, we will only ever do the things that we WANT to do. So, it is more accurate and helpful to understand this in its proper sequence. The "WANT" always comes before the "WILL". Our wants activate and energize our will. Your will only ever achieves for you those things that you truly WANT to obtain.

Your will is only capable of obtaining for you what it is currently producing for you. Which is determined by your current wants. For your will to produce a different result it must be activated by different or more powerful wants.

So, you must understand and embrace that the WANT must come before the WILL. You don't really have WILL Power. What you really have is **WANT POWER!!!**

Let's be honest. We do the things we do, because we WANT to do them. Plain and simple. This is the most honest way for us to take ownership for our actions. You see, until we take ownership for something we do not have the right to do with it as we please. However, once you OWN something, it is yours. And once you own it, you have the right to do with it whatever it is you decide. Because it is YOURS.

One powerful way to establish this ownership is to accept the reality that everything we do; we do because somewhere inside us we WANT to do it. When we want to do something then we will do it. To the degree that we want it, is to the degree that we will do it. Here you can see that the will is clearly preceded by the want. This is also closely tied to Rule #7 "Your Intentionality Determines Your Potentiality".

One clever and simple test to help prove this truth is to think of a food or activity that you love. Hold this in your mind, then by using your will power, immediately cause yourself to stop liking that food or that activity. Because if it is true that you really have a will power, then you can surely will yourself to dislike something that you currently love. Or, to like something that you currently do not like, simply by the sheer power of your will.

If you try this, you will find it is a pointless exercise. I have asked many people to do this as part of illustrating this truth and they routinely respond by saying things like: "Why would I **want** to do that?" or "I don't really **want** to stop liking this, etc….."

These responses expose the fact that what we truly have is want power, not will power. Our will proceeds from our wants. Our willingness proceeds from our "wantingness". What we want, we have the willingness to do. Conversely, what we do not want, we will not do or will struggle doing. Our will follows and is energized by our wants.

It is important at this point to clarify that our "wants" are not directly tied exclusively to those things we enjoy or desire. It is incorrect to believe that we only want to do things that are pleasurable or enjoyable. Because the truth is that many times we have to do things that we don't want to do, but we do them anyway. However, even in this, we still do them because we want to. Not because we enjoy it, but because we have to, so we want to. Have I confused you? Stay with me…

The truth is that wanting is just wanting, it can be motivated by different factors. Even things that we may not necessarily enjoy doing, we still do because at some level we want to do them. Always remember that ultimately, we ONLY do the things we WANT to do.

Pain/Pleasure Principle

The Pain/Pleasure principle states that fundamentally all human actions are driven by either our desire to seek pleasure or avoid pain. Therefore, some of our wants are driven by responsibility, duty, fear of consequence, etc. While other wants are driven by what we find pleasurable, convenient, enjoyable.

The pain/pleasure principle is key to understanding the psychology of what drives human actions. Fundamentally, we do what we do because we have a WANT to do it. Because we WANT to seek some perceived pleasure, or we WANT to avoid some perceived pain. But in both cases the WANT is the key point. Do you understand now?

Our wants are driven by our perceptions, imaginations, and associations of what causes us pain and pleasure

You cannot escape the fact that ultimately, **you only do things that you want to do**. Even if you may not like doing them. You do them because you want to. This is a very empowering realization; The things we do, we do because we WANT to do them. PERIOD!!!

But you may say, I don't really want to go to work. I only go to work because I have to. Well, it is precisely because **you have to**, that **you want to**. And that want is what activates your willingness to get up and grudgingly go to work.

If you smoke it is because you want to smoke. If you are overweight, it is because you want to eat the foods you eat and do not want to exercise or diet accordingly. Be honest with yourself. Own it. By the way, it's ok because these are all choices we make. It is your right to choose (Empowerment Rule #5). You have the power and right to choose the things you want for yourself.

This is not about passing judgement or being critical. But we must be honest with ourselves because we gain nothing by being deceived. Our empowerment, in a large way, lies in our ability to be honest and act in the fullest truth. There is power in the truth. There is weakness in deception.

If you want to smoke, do so and enjoy it. Even if you know it will bring health concerns. Do it with pleasure as this is your choice. Why choose to do things and then judge yourself or be torn within yourself? Do what you want and enjoy doing it. Remember no one can tell you what to choose. Be certain and confident in your choices. Enjoy them, revel in them. Why would you do otherwise? They are YOUR choices and no one else's.

However, if you want to change, then change. Just do it. It is all part of becoming more intentional in every area of your life. Being intentional and purposeful in every situation and in every moment, is the true hallmark of the empowered person. Being present in the moment and clear about your purpose and intentions is how you harness and direct your conscious power and unleash your Empowered Self.

If you want good health, then make it a point to develop strong "wants" to do the things that will make this happen in your life. Be certain within yourself that you want to live a healthy life. Start saying to yourself "I want to be healthy". Acknowledge this as a certain and confident determination. Begin with asserting your intention. Because your intentionality determines your potentiality (Rule #7).

The first person you MUST convince of anything is YOU. Once you become convinced of and establish strong wants, this activates the power of your willingness. This process of creating strong wants is what will energize you to accomplish the things you want by way of activating your WILL.

If you want a better relationship, develop "wants" to do the things that will grow the relationship. Want to be nicer, more understanding, more complimentary, etc. If you want to be successful in your career, then continually develop "wants" to do the things that will advance your career. Want to be on time, want to embrace doing the work with a positive attitude, want to achieve, despite obstacles or frustrations. Want to avoid complaining, etc.…Does this make sense? Focus on developing the "want to" so you can then have the "will to".

Dealing with the "should do"

Here is a conflict that in some ways we all experience…. We have things that we do (because we want to do them), but in our conscience (right or wrong) we feel that there are different things that we "should" do. So, on the one hand, we have the things we do, because we want to do them. And on the other hand, we have a list of "should" that we believe for whatever reason we should do instead.

This internal dilemma creates conflict and, in some cases, deep psychological turmoil within us. We can become confused, frustrated, angry, depressed, etc. Because we see the things that we DO, and realize they are contrary to the things we know we SHOULD DO. Yes, this can cause deep conflict within us.

The empowered person is intentional and effectively deals with resolving this dilemma. The empowered YOU has the courage to settle the matter and intentionally decide to want the things you know you should want. There is no dilemma, no inner conflict. Just purposeful, intentional wants, desires and actions.

You are MASTER of YOU. You determine and inform your wants, and this informs and energizes your will. And to the degree that you do this it causes your actions to be in perfect alignment. Now there is no conflict or inner judgement. You are acting in line with your true intentions, desires, and purposes.

But as with everything in life there is a process. And every process involves time. So, you must be certain and patient. There is also the element of prior subconscious programming that comes into play when you examine your actions and try to determine the diving factor (pain/pleasure/programming). We will discuss this in more detail in Empowerment Rule #5.

So now, the big question remains. How can you turn a "should" into a "want"? What faculty do you possess that can make this happen? The faculty you possess that enables you to turn your "should" into "wants", which in turn activates your WILL, causing you to act consistent with your intentional wants is …… your IMAGINATION. Yes, your Imagination.

"Imagination rules the world"
Napoleon

The Power of Imagination

By use of our imagination we find the **KEY** to help us consciously and intentionally determine our wants and line them up with our "should". By using your imagination, you can so inform your mind to seek the things you want to do. By intentionally defining what is painful or pleasurable for you. Yes, you can effectively determine your pain/pleasure perceptions by way of utilizing your imagination in more intentional and directed ways.

What is more painful, to not eat that food or to eat that food? Well, currently it is pleasurable to my taste buds. It tastes "good", so I do it to seek pleasure. But by way of my imagination I can inform my thinking to associate that particular food (whatever it may be) with negative outcomes. This food makes me fat, this food is filled with harmful preservatives, eating this food hurts me, etc.

What is more pleasurable, to smoke that cigarette or not smoke that cigarette? Well, "I smoke because I think it is cool and elevates my self-view". "But by way of my imagination I can picture black, cancerous billows of smoke filling my lungs with every puff. I can literally feel my lung tissues shrivel with every puff of carcinogen filled smoke, etc....."

The point here is that if you effectively and intentionally activate your imagination, you can create new and powerful negative or positive associations of your own intention. New mental associations that suit your true wants and desires. New mental associations that will create in you new and different WANTS that activate your WILL enabling you to make the changes you desire.

The EMPOWERED individual has the ability to turn their "should" into a "want" by means of their imagination and intentionality. Yes, by effectively directing your imagination you can intentionally inform and determine your new wants which will set your new WILL.... which will drive your new actions. Once a want is firmly planted in the conscious and subconscious mind this will result in a willingness that eventually produces your desired result.

If you are not yet convinced of how powerful your imagination is, consider the familiar condition of acrophobia, the fear of high places. You can have two people standing on the same high ledge, right next to each another. One person is perfectly fine suffering no qualms or fears. Totally comfortable maybe even excited, experiencing high, positive emotions. While the other person that suffers from acrophobia is experiencing an uncontrollable and paralyzing fear. Causing them severe negative emotions of fear and dread.

What is the difference? They are both standing in the exact same place, experiencing the same physical reality, yet their responses are completely different. The difference is the effect their imagination is having on them. One person's imagination has run away with them in a negative, uncontrollable, disempowered way. Causing them sheer panic and other negative physiological effects.

They are in no different danger other than what their imaginations have concocted. The difference is how both their imaginations processed the exact same situation yet come up with two totally different outcomes. Both yielding completely different physical and emotional states.

By active and intentional use of your imagination you have the POWERFUL faculty needed to so inform your thinking in any way you intend. In any way that suits your true desires. You can create new mental associations of your choosing by using your creative and imaginative faculty to inform your WANTS.

So, if you want better or desire to be better you must be willing and eager to be DIFFERENT…to CHANGE…And you do this by consciously utilizing your imagination to initiate the change you desire.

"It is the imagination and not the will which is the dominating faculty of man. It is a serious mistake to advise people to train their wills; they should learn to control and direct their imaginations"

Emile Coue'

Empowerment Habit:

Be Creative and Imaginative

"The world is but a canvas to the imagination"
Henry David Thoreau

I AM… Creative and Imaginative. I put my mind to the things I want to solve or realize. I visualize the outcomes as desired. I use my imagination to create effective pain/pleasure associations of my own intentional desires in order to establish the wants that energize my will.

It is your imagination that can spark and enable you to move in any direction you desire. It is a powerful faculty that most of us allow to lay dormant. We fail to realize the power of this amazing capability that we all possess. And therefore, sadly, we disregard and underestimate it.

Think about it. What is the first step in realizing anything different than what you currently see, do, or get? The very FIRST step is to IMAGINE the new thing, behavior, or result that you consciously and intentionally WANT.

Your imagination is the KEY….it opens the door to those things unseen that you wish to experience, realize, or become. Using your imagination is not child's play. It is EMPOWERMENT 101.

Our imagination knows no bounds. It is through your imagination that you have access to the wellspring of infinite possibilities. It is in your imagination that you are boundless and limitless. From imagination springs all of the wonder that we dare to create, manifest, realize, and experience. Imagination is the Garden of God. Our imagination sparks the creative force that the universe must obey. It is by means of our creative and imaginative faculties, we have access to the field of infinite potential.

"Logic will get you from A to B.
Imaginations will take you everywhere."
Albert Einstein

Anything imagined can become realized. This is why the only word the universe and your subconscious mind knows is "YES" (Empowerment Rule #10).

The problem is that over the course of our lives we have been so effectively brain washed to stop using our imagination and to instead become more "realistic". How many times have we heard this? "Come now, be realistic". Or "You have to be realistic about this" etc.....

We have been programmed into believing we should be realistic about things. We have elevated this concept of being realistic to the level of a virtue. When in fact, being realistic is a limiting and disempowering VICE.

To be realistic means to accept what currently is and no more. The problem with this limiting mindset is that it keeps us bound to what we currently see, do, or get. Why would you want to encourage someone to be realistic when what they truly desire in most cases is YET to be realized? Most of the time what we truly desire is something different than our current reality.

So, to be realistic is to accept and settle for the very things we want to change. I say NO, be unrealistic. Set your sights on those hopes and ambitions that are yet to be realized. Be hopeful and imaginary…our hope is what drives us forward.

"Where there is no hope in the future.
There is no power in the present"
John Maxwell

I am not suggesting you totally ignore the current reality to the point where you fail to deal responsibly with the here and now. You must deal with and responsibly handle the current reality. But, you can also set your mind on a future reality that you truly desire to experience and realize. Because all attainment starts in the imagination does it not?

What I am saying is that we DO NOT have to settle for the current reality. Our current reality is merely the objectified outcome of our prior mindset, beliefs, desires, and actions. It is an echo of the past. The empowered individual understands and embraces this truth. They accept and deal responsibly with the present, yet always looks forward with a hopeful, imaginary attitude. Knowing that what we imagine today can be real for us tomorrow.

You must not allow yourself to be bound by the current reality if what you truly desire is something different. Simply use your current situation as the starting point on your journey to the next thing you decide to pursue. All realization begins in the imagination. You must imagine in order to realize. Do not let what you now see, determine what you will continue to be.

We are fundamentally designed to always desire beyond what we currently have. We all possess this intrinsic need to keep striving for more, always wanting, and desiring more. This is the reason why no matter what we have, even if it at first seemed marvelous, eventually dulls and then, we naturally long for something else, something different, something more.

This tendency should not cause us to be ungrateful for our current lot in life. To the contrary. Having a grateful and appreciative heart must always be our starting point. We must live in a constant state of gratitude coupled with the knowing that any longing we possess we can and should pursue if it flows from our deepest desires and intentions. But the starting point should always be the grateful "now".

You have the capability and dare I say, responsibility, to continually realize and create new realties in your life. Life is intended to be a seeking, a growing, an expanding. It is on this journey of growing where you will find your true ongoing fulfillment. Because everything that is here and now has prepared you for what you can become or experience tomorrow and beyond.

Not only is this a basic human longing, to keep growing and expanding. But we also have been given the capability to make this happen. We have been designed for this purpose. And our imagination is the primary faculty we must embrace and utilize as part of this process. As imagination is the starting point to all realization.

No matter how far our desired reality may appear to be. In your imagination anything can be brought closer. You must visualize and imagine the things you desire as these are powerful gateways to impress the subconscious mind. Which then actively works towards the materialization of these impressions. We are to lead imaginary lives backed by the actions that can realize those imaginings.

"First comes thought; then organization of that thought, into ideas and plans; then transformation of those plans into reality. The beginning, as you will observe, is in your imagination."

Napoleon Hill

Empowerment Rule #4

You Have To Give To Get

"The basic rule of free enterprise: You must give, in order to get"
Scott Alexander

You will only ever receive to the degree that you are willing to graciously give. You have to give, to get. At first this appears to be an irrational paradox. How is it that you get when you give? When you give, don't you instantly have less? Well, to understand this empowerment rule you must first develop a **mindset of abundance and generosity** coupled with an **attitude of gratitude and appreciation**. This is foundational to living a truly giving, prosperous, and empowered life.

The Mindset of Abundance

You must cultivate a deep belief that there is abundance. That there is plenty to go around. You must operate from the empowered mindset of abundance. NEVER allow the disempowering, limiting, and wrong ideal of scarcity to be part of your thinking. You see, scarcity is a myth and a lie. The truth is that there is abundance and plenty of all, and for all.

One reason why we do not have a more giving spirit could be because deep inside we may be victim to this mindset of "limited supply". Where we believe that if we give to someone else, there will logically be less for ourselves. That if someone else has more, there will naturally be less for us. Or that if someone else is successful, there will be less opportunity for us to be successful. This notion of limited supply and opportunity is disempowering, selfish, and WRONG!!!

You must embrace the belief that there is abundance, unlimited supply. Not only of physical things and resources, but also of opportunities, relationships, and even the invisible things like love, acceptance, joy, patience, understanding, etc. There is unlimited supply.

We live in a world of abundance and of infinite potentiality (more later on this concept). Even if at times there may appear to be a limited supply of things or resources. By the application of intentionality, imagination, and creativity, we can develop new technology, resources, or processes that will cause the once "limited" supply to become multiplied and therefore increase.

But you may ask, "What about those individuals who live in poverty and want". "Doesn't that support the notion of scarcity?" Well, these situations exist because those that live in poverty and lack are being subjected to that experience by themselves or by more powerful forces who desire to subject them. And this for political or other social-economic reasons. It is because those in power, or in a position to change this, cannot, or will not, embrace the notion of giving in order to get. They have other controlling, selfish, evil, or limiting agendas.

There is more than plenty to go around. The technological and natural resources are over abundant. They simply have to be utilized for the greater good as opposed to solely for the profit and control of the wealthy and powerful. But, this is not a book about politics or social order. So, I will not discuss these things further. However, it is important to touch on this in order to dispel the notion of limited resources.

There is abundance. Where abundance is not experienced it is because of a lack of intentionality, creativity, or resources and this, due to controlling, limiting, or plain evil intentions.

The Mindset of Generosity

Many of us live with this limiting notion that "I must hold on tightly to what I have, or risk losing it". "Because if I lose it or give it away, I may never have it again". Wrongly believing that there is a limited supply, we selfishly hold on to what we have. This attitude is limiting and disempowering. It must be replaced with an attitude of gratitude and generosity.

We are to hold on to things not with a closed, tight fist, but with an open, trusting hand. An open hand gives but can also receive. This should be our heart attitude. The only way to receive more is with an open hand, not with a tightly clenched fist.

Living with open and trusting hands allows others to receive as well as allowing you to also receive more. Upon an open and trusting hand much more will surely pass. There will be much more to give, and much more to receive.

"Only by giving are you able to receive more than you already have"
Jim Rohn

Sowing and Reaping

This empowerment rule reflects the law of sowing and reaping. There are two specific principles of the law of sowing and reaping that always apply. The first is the **principle of duplication**...what you sow, you will reap. If you plant apple seeds you will get apples. You never get oranges when you plant apple seeds. The type of seed planted always determines the type of plant that will eventually grow and be harvested. The reaping is always of the same kind as what is sown. This is called the principle of duplication.

The second principle is the **principle of multiplication**. Which means that if you plant one apple seed you don't get back a harvest that only yields one seed. You will reap an apple tree that yields many apples, each one containing many more seeds. The reaping is always far greater in measure than what is sown. The harvest, when it happens, is always greatly multiplied.

When sowing and reaping the principles of Duplication and Multiplication will always have their effect. This is also the case when you apply Empowerment Rule #4 Give to Get. You will always get back in kind to what you give and in far greater measure than you have given. Always remember this.

What happens when you give? You are now expressing an attitude of abundance because you appreciate what you have to the extent that you are willing to share and to give. Once you give, this automatically benefits someone else. As they can also experience the "having". Since they also now "have", they can become inspired and encouraged to start producing it for themselves.

Since you already have it, you have already experienced how to procure it. This enables you to keep on producing and sharing in this spirit of abundance. You are also not concerned to give of yourself because you know you can keep filling up with more love, kindness, gratitude, appreciation, advice, wisdom, etc.

Whatever it is you are giving away, you will naturally and effortlessly produce to a greater degree. Because you now acting in a spirit of generosity and abundance.

In giving you automatically receive. What is it that you receive? A sense of satisfaction, accomplishment, of blessing. A sense of power for good. A settled peace that you have acted generously and selflessly. By your actions someone else can experience a gift of kindness, love, money, food, gratitude, etc.

"It is more blessed to give than to receive"
Acts 20:35

Be willing to give boundlessly, consistently, and effortlessly because you will only receive in relation to and in greater proportion to what you are willing to graciously give. So, give of your time, your attention, your best intentions, patience, love, kindness, understanding, helping hand, money, resources, etc.

Develop a mindset of wanting to "super-serve" others. This starts with simply desiring the best for all people. Always wishing well for all those around you. Always seeing and expecting the best in others. This must be your continual mindset towards everyone. Even those individuals you may not even particularly like. Because what credit is it to you if you only appreciate and like those that appreciate and like you? GIVE!!! To all people.

Here is a practical way to understand the rule of GIVE to GET

You want appreciation?
Give appreciation

You want respect?
Give respect.

You want love?
Give love

You want more money?
Add more value.

You want to be understood?
Be understanding.

If you can help someone out, then do so. If someone on the street needs $5 and you have $5 in your pocket……GIVE!!!

If someone you know has an immediate need that involves $200 and you have that money to give…GIVE!!!

If someone in your circle of relation has a deep need and they need $5,000. But, you are not in a financial position to help with that amount, then give them heartfelt sympathy. Give them any wise counsel that may help to lighten their load or to find a solution to their problem…. GIVE!!!

We have an outstanding debt to others to continually give the best of ourselves. To treat others better than we expect to be treated. To super-serve others. We will only ever get in proportion to what we willingly, selflessly, lovingly, and abundantly give to others. The three EMPOWERMENT HABITS that follow will enable you to live out this Empowerment Rule of GIVE To GET.

Empowerment Habit:

Be Grateful

"Gratitude is not only the greatest of virtues, but the parent of all others"
Cicero

I AM…Grateful. I know that everything I have, I have received. Therefore, I continually give thanks for all I have been graciously privileged to have and enjoy.

Attitude of Gratitude

The foundation for a truly prosperous life is to live in a continual state of gratitude. A person that lacks the ability to appreciate, to be grateful, will never experience true abundance. As they can never have enough. Even if they acquire a mountain of "things", they will still be in lack. Because they are unable to appreciate and be grateful for what they have already received. The attitude of ingratitude inevitably results in an unfulfilled, sad, empty, and disempowered life.

True fulfillment can only happen on the inside. No number of physical things can fill the inside void that is created when we have an attitude of ingratitude and lack of appreciation. The issue is not the number of things acquired. The issue is the ability to appreciate and be grateful for what you currently have.

"Gratitude is the healthiest of all human emotions. The more you express gratitude for what you have, the more likely you will have even more to express gratitude for"
Zig Ziglar

The empowered individual always starts from the place of gratitude. This attitude of gratitude sets the stage for a more fulfilled life. It is only in this state that one can truly experience lasting fulfillment and joy.

First, we must be honest and acknowledge the reality that we all have a natural, built in inclination towards ingratitude. Yes, this is our natural tendency. We are all prone to ignore or overlook the many daily benefits life graciously provides us. Simply put, we tend to take things for granted. This is our natural condition….one of ingratitude.

"Ingratitude is treason to mankind"
James Thompson

This is the sad but true reality. We all have this natural condition that predisposes us to being dismissive and unappreciative of the many wonderful things we are blessed to have and enjoy daily. From the sun that shines on us and warms us; to the soft breeze that cools us; to the beauty that nature provides us as our everyday scenery. The work that we are fortunate to have that provides for ourselves and our families. The loved ones that grace our lives. The comfortable bed we enjoy every night, etc. The list is long….

This is not a judgement it is simply a fact. We do not possess the ability to be continually grateful. Our human tendency is towards the opposite, ingratitude. We do not have the capability to fully appreciate and be thankful. Therefore, gratefulness is a habit that must be cultivated with a high degree of intentionality and persistence. It is a muscle that we must continually condition and build up.

Knowing these things, it is only fitting and appropriate that our response be to desire to develop a habit of gratitude. When we find ourselves in a critical or ungrateful attitude, we should consciously trigger ourselves to focus on the things we should be grateful for. This should become an automatic response that we condition ourselves to perform.

We must see the world through eyes that continually values and appreciates all the wonderful things, and all the unique life experiences that we are fortunate to have.

You can rightly say that there is magic in every moment. As every day is a miracle that has been brought forth for our benefit, to enjoy and appreciate. When we see life this way it changes our naturally dismissive and critical attitudes. We can then develop a more lovely and grateful disposition.

Thank You

An effective antidote to this negative, disempowering habit of taking things for granted is to be grateful and say, "thank you". Yes, we are to give thanks often and in every situation. Because, if you really think about it, what do you have that you did not receive? Everything you have, you have received. And the appropriate and correct response whenever receiving something is to say, "thank you". To be grateful.

"What do you have that you did not receive, and if you did receive it, then why do you boast as though you had not?"

1 Cor 4:7

Do not miss the many opportunities you are presented each day to recognize and appreciate others for what they do and who they are. So, we should say "thank you" as often as possible to all the people we interact with daily.

Also, make it a continual practice to simply say thank you silently throughout your day as you acknowledge and appreciate many of the daily blessing and benefits that you routinely enjoy.

Even in those things you have worked for, that you believe you rightly deserve as result of your efforts. Well, even in those things, you still received them; so, you should give thanks. Where did you get the strength and the ability to achieve them? Did you work for that? Or was that given to you? Give Thanks.

To teach this lesson to my children I remind them to go all the way back to their birth. And to ask; "What did you do to contribute to being born? What did you do to earn this most precious gift of life?" The answer is that we contributed nothing to the most significant event in our lives. Our creation and birth. So, this provides clear evidence that our very lives are a gift. A gift that we did nothing to deserve. And everything else that flows from this undeserved life are continual gifts that we should be GRATEFUL for.

"Be thankful in all circumstances
for this is Gods will for you."
1Thessalonians 5:18

Every iota of this life are gifts that we receive. That we should appreciate, enjoy, and be grateful for. If by our negative or ungrateful attitudes we choose to not appreciate them, then we demonstrate that we are not worthy of the gift. Gratitude is the greatest of all virtues…then follows humility.

Since gratitude is a most powerful emotion we should start and end each day with thoughts of gratitude. Be conscious to make your VERY FIRST thought upon waking one of gratitude and appreciation. As soon as your alarm goes off and you awake, in that very moment, instead of allowing any random thought to enter your mind, immediately think of something you are grateful for. Maybe list two or three things. Try this habit and you will find that it is an affective and powerful way to start the day with a more positive disposition.

Gratitude is like a muscle.
As you exercise it, it will become stronger

Develop this same habit when you go to bed at night. Let those last conscious thoughts of your day be ones of gratitude and appreciation. Think about the positive things you experienced or encountered during the day. Find the small things that you may have missed, dismissed, or overlooked. Cultivate thankfulness in the final minutes of each day.

If you practice daily prayers or meditations make sure to include counting your blessings as you focus on all the things you are grateful for. You will find that as you become more and more grateful this changes your disposition in a positive and empowering way.

"The Struggle ends when gratitude begins"
Neale Donald Walsh

Empowerment Habit:

Be Appreciative

"Appreciate what you have, before it turns into what you had"

I AM…Appreciative. I genuinely appreciate all the people and things in my life. This heart attitude fills my life with joy and abundance.

The Empowering Effect of Appreciation

Do you realize that you possess the ability to make things more valuable? That you have within you the capacity to instantly create more abundance in your life? That you can create more value and worth in all the things you possess, and in all the people you interact with? You do. And the way you do this is simply by choosing to **appreciate more**.

When you appreciate something or someone, what happens? That person or thing increases in their worth. They become more valuable to you. They appreciate. Yes, you have the power to make things more valuable simply by appreciating them more.

This is a life changing realization. You can create and experience a greater sense of abundance in your life simply by appreciating people and things more. You do not need a special system, tool, or process to do this. You simply need to make the continual, intentional choice to appreciate the people and things in your life more. You can apply this to everything….it is like magic:

Appreciate your wife…and, she will become more valuable to you.
Appreciate your job…and, it will become more valuable to you.
Appreciate your health….and, it will become more valuable to you.
Appreciate your friends…and, they will become more valuable to you
Appreciate your home….and, it will become more valuable to you.

Anything you appreciate increases in worth and becomes more valuable to you.

You have the amazing ability to create value simply by your intentional choice to appreciate more. This mindset of appreciation sets the stage for a life of abundance. A practical and lovely way for you to get more out of this life is to cause the things you already possess or experience to become more valuable. And you do this simply by applying the **magical power of appreciation**.

Remember, appreciation is simply a choice that you make. You hold within yourself the power to make the people and things in your life more valuable to you. Simply by your intentional and persistent choice to appreciate them more.

So, choose to appreciate the people in your personal and professional circles. Make it a daily practice in your prayers, meditations, or anytime you think about it, to number in your mind the people and things you appreciate. Send them a positive wave of your intentional, honest, loving, thoughts of gratitude and appreciation.

As you appreciate them, you will now see them in a greater light. This will positively affect how you interact with and project towards them. You are benefiting them by your continual choice to be appreciative. You are already "giving" them something by this intentional choice you have made to appreciate them more. And this immediately sets up a more prosperous situation, and the relationships will inevitably grow.

"You get the best out of others when you give the best of yourself"
Harvey S. Firestone

Another positive effect of appreciating people and things more is that you will become more inclined to take better care of them. We all take better care of those things we value. We look after them, keep them safe, and treat them well. We are more mindful of them. Yes, as you appreciate people and things more, you will naturally tend to treat them better. You will treat them with more love, patience, and care. This is a wonderful form of GIVING. And you will GET back a greater sense of joy and fulfillment.

A practical way to develop this appreciation mindset is to continually practice focusing on the positive qualities of the people and things that you want to appreciate. What is it about them that you admire or like? What qualities (physical, emotional, personality, etc.) do you appreciate about them? Place the positives foremost in your thinking as you interact with them. This will inevitably create a stronger connection and will set the stage for more empowered, meaningful, and fulfilling relations.

Always choose to see people in their best light. Magnify their positive qualities.

At the same time, you must resist any tendency or inclination to be a fault finder, or negative critic. Because this attitude has the very opposite effect. It diminishes, devalues, and deteriorates the thing or relationship. When you are negative or critical of people or things you are robbing them of value. And this sets in motion a negative downward spiral of depreciation and devaluing.

Appreciation is a powerful and effective form of giving. You are giving more when you consistently hold people and things in a high regard. By doing so you are creating abundance in your relationships and possessions. So, cultivate an attitude that is continually inclined towards appreciation and gratefulness. And when you couple this with a mindset of abundance and generosity you now have set the stage for a truly EMPOWERED and PROSPEROUS life.

Attitude of Gratitude
&
Appreciation

+

Mindset of Abundance
&
Generosity

=

EMPOWERED & PROSPEROUS LIFE

Empowerment Habit:

Be Complimentary

"I can live for two months on a good compliment"
Mark Twain

I AM…. Complimentary. I know that an honest compliment can warn the heart and touch the soul of another. I will empower others by my habit of finding opportunities to pay them kind compliments.

A simple habit to develop that has great positive impact and provides another way for you to GIVE is to continually find reasons to compliment others.

A genuine compliment has the power to make someone feel better about themselves and their situation in life. It is a sure way to bring someone an immediate smile and a positive feeling. A heartfelt and honest compliment is a powerful gift that you can always give to others at no cost to you, but of great value to the recipient.

Think about something complimentary that someone has said to you. Does it not bring you confidence or comfort whenever you think of it? Of course, it does. You never know if your compliment will be something of such positive effect that the recipient will carry it with them all their lives. Paying compliments is a powerful, easy, and effective way of giving.

When paying compliments, you must be honest. Don't do it simply for the sake of paying a compliment, but because it is true and because you really mean it. Find reasons to recognize and compliment others.

Simple complimentary comments like; "Nice tie. Love your hair. That is a great idea. You look extra special today. You are very clever. I am very impressed by how you did that, you look awesome", etc. will go a long way in making others feel special and appreciated.

To your family members you should choose to often say kind and meaningful things like:

I love you very much.
I think you are amazing.
You are so important to me.
You are the most understanding person I know.
I appreciate all the things you do for me.

At work choose to often say positive things like:

I was really impressed with the way you handled that.
That was an excellent suggestion.
Well done.
You are amazing at doing this job.
You really make a positive difference in this company.
We are very fortunate to have you on our team.

Everyone wants to feel Important and Appreciated

We are all looking for continual validation, for confirmation that we matter. I truly believe that the foundational human emotional need that we all share is the need to feel IMPORTANT and APPRECIATED. When you compliment others, you are giving them something truly special. Because, by way of your compliment, you are helping them find that validation that we all long for. You are making them feel IMPORTANT and APPRECIATED. What a wonderful gift you have given and what a privilege it is to be that powerful gift giver.

"We make a living by what we get,
but we make a life by what we give"
Winston Churchill

Empowerment Rule #5

You Have The POWER To CHOOSE

"You are not a product of circumstances you are a product of your choices"

It is in Empowerment rule #5 that we find the true seed of our POWER. The power to experience and realize a life of your own intentional choosing. The essence of empowerment lies in your right and ability to make choices in every area of your life.

An important objective of the empowerment journey is to gain right understanding. Put more simply, to know more truth. If we are not embracing and acting in the truth, then we are deceived. To the degree that we are not living in the fullness of truth, is to the degree that we are living in deception. There is no other way around it.

Living in a state of deception puts us in a disempowered condition. The way to break out of deceptions is to discover and embrace more truth and then to faithfully apply it in our lives. This is the formula for continued empowerment.

As we gain more truth, we become more enlightened. We can see things in a greater and clearer light. It is in this greater and clearer light that we can see, appreciate, and understand more, and more fully. As we become more aware and accepting of greater truth, we inevitably lead more honest lives. Living more honest and truth filled lives is necessary for our empowerment. There is no power in lies and deception, even if well intentioned. It is only in the truth that we find freedom and therefore, power.

"You shall know the truth and the truth shall set you free"
John 8:32

In this empowerment rule we discover a most powerful truth. That we have the right and the power to choose in every situation. And that it is our choices that ultimately determine the course and content of our lives.

Embracing this truth is powerful because it allows you to immediately move from a position of victim to victor. From innocent bystander to the intentional and active causative agent in your life. It takes you from feeling controlled and manipulated to realizing that YOU are the one in control. It places the power where it truly resides. NOT in outside situations or circumstances, but in YOU.

When you realize and accept that in life you have the power to CHOOSE, the doors of opportunity and possibility open wide. Embrace this truth and your life will forever change. This is truth.

"It is your decisions, not your conditions that determine your destiny"
Tony Robbins

We make choices in every area of our lives, every day, and in varied ways. Who we have relations with, what we wear, eat, say, and do. Where we work, where we live. The car we drive. Etc. Our lives are filled with choices of every sort. And with every choice we make there is a corresponding consequence. Both short term and long term.

Some choices carry little consequence some greater etc. The important truth we must accept and embrace is that we are experiencing the results and consequences of our collective choices. And as such, we must take full responsibility for our lot in this life.

But some will say, "I don't choose all the things that happen to me. Some things happen to me outside of my own choosing". Well, if we could exhaustively and accurately trace the path of our decisions and choices over time we would find that any situation we find ourselves in was inevitably brought about by the collective and progressive series of choices we made along the way.

Like it or not, there is no escaping the fact that our lives are 100% a product of all our collective choices. We are, every day, and in every way, experiencing the effects and consequences of all our choices.

But let's, for the sake of argument, say that some things happen to us that we had no participation at all in choosing. That they just happen to us "out of the blue". Well, even in those situations, we still have the power to make choices and decisions regarding how we react and respond to those situations. Because you possess the power to choose how to receive and interpret every situation and circumstance you encounter in life. You have the power to choose your perspectives and responses, no matter what the situation may be.

"Between stimulus and response there is a space.
In that space is our power to choose our response.
In our response lies our growth and our freedom."
Viktor E. Frankl

So, we understand that in ANY and EVERY situation there is that space of time between the event and our response to that event. And it is in that space of time that we can access our power. The power to choose our perspective, attitude, and response. And it is this choosing that will determine our empowered path forward.

Additionally, it is important to understand that situations and circumstances in life do not interpret themselves. And, more importantly, they do NOT come with inherent, objective, labels that you must mandatorily apply or accept. The truth is that ALL the things that happen in life are inherently NEUTRAL in meaning and purpose. Because it is not until YOU process, interpret, and give meaning to any situation that it now becomes meaningful and purposeful for YOU.

It's YOUR Label Maker

A truly empowering realization is that, in life, YOU do the labeling. YOU have the power and ability to define situations in ANY way YOU choose. This is a KEY Empowerment concept.

You can rightly say that every situation you experience is presented to you like the proverbial "cup filled ½ way". You can choose to see it as half full, or half empty. Both perspectives are correct. But they are polar opposites as to the effect they will have on your attitudes, emotions, actions, and ultimately, your outcomes.

Yes, every situation is inherently neutral and void of any specific meaning until YOU bring the meaning and purpose to it by CHOOSING your perspective and interpretation of it. It is for YOU to choose how you will see and receive ANY situation. You apply the labels. And only YOU can do this for yourself as this is your sovereign right.

Life just happens, you get to DEFINE it. This is a KEY understanding that when embraced results in a breakthrough in your empowerment journey.

NO situation comes with an inherent label of "good" or "bad". You create and apply the labels. And since it is you that does the labeling, you can choose to avoid the typical negative labeling that you have been conditioned and programmed to accept.

"For there is nothing either good or bad,
but thinking makes it so."
Shakespeare

The reason you must avoid the obvious labeling of "good" or "bad" is because these are just subjective labels. In anything "good" you can find a "bad". In anything "bad" you can find a "good". How many people have won a million dollars and it ruined their lives? How many have found fame and fortune only to experience its curse? Conversely, how many people have experienced tragedy but became positively transformed as a result? How many challenges and difficulties have led to wonderful outcomes. And how many wonderful situations have led to tragedy.

So, you see, things you may label as good, can be for bad, and things you may label as bad, can be for good. Labels, labels, labels. All labels that you get to assign and define. YOU CHOOSE.

Therefore, you must not allow yourself to automatically fall in line with to the common negative interpretations and disempowering labels. You hold they keys to interpreting life however you choose. And you should choose to assign the meaning and purpose that most benefits you. That most empowers you to live a positive and fulfilled life. That is your power, if you choose to embrace and apply it.

Some may persist and say: "But, aren't there situations that are clearly issues or problems?" NO, there are simply situations. How you perceive and label them is TOTALLY your choice. And whatever you choose, will be true for you. Because this is what you will accept as true and thus realize the effect of in your life.

Below is a great example of how in our choosing we are both justified and subjected to the effect of that corresponding choice.

Story of Twin Boys:

**Two twin boys were raised by an alcoholic father.
One grew up to be an alcoholic
and when asked what happened he said,
"I watched my father".**

**The other grew up and never drank in his life.
When he was asked what happened he said,
"I watched my father".**

**Two boys, same father.
Two different perspectives.
Two different outcomes.**

Your choices in life will determine your destiny.

Always remember that regardless how any situation may be typically perceived by other people. How YOU receive and perceive it is YOUR own individual choice. You can decide if a situation will cause you to serve it, creating in you negative and disempowering thoughts and emotions. Or if the situation will serve to empower you, by finding a positive purpose in it. One of your own choosing.

John's House Burned Down

Let me give you a hypothetical example of the power of choosing your perspective and corresponding response. Let's say John's house burned down and he lost every single worldly possession. He lost absolutely EVERYTHING. His pictures, family heirlooms, TVs, phones, clothes, jewelry, etc.

Most people would agree that this is a BIG problem for John. They would promptly label the situation as a real tragedy. However, no matter how many people choose to label his situation as a "problem". John still retains the power to decide that for him, it is NOT a problem. He can choose to decide that, for him, it is a blessing and an opportunity. He can choose to say.... "I survived the fire, I am still alive. I am grateful, and more than that, I thought I was defined by my possessions. But now I realize that I am NOT my possessions, and that I am NOT defined by my stuff. I now realize that I am greater than all of that. And now, because of this "tragedy" I feel a greater sense of freedom. I am more grateful for my life. Plus, I know that I can look forward to eventually getting newer and better "stuff".

You see, John has turned his tragedy into triumph simply by choosing to do so. In this situation, he could have chosen the "obvious" and "popular" label of seeing his situation as a tragedy, as a devastating problem. And he would have been rightly justified in his feelings of grief, hopelessness, anger, frustration, etc. Who could blame him for choosing that response?

But, he also has the power to choose with an Empowered mindset. He has the freedom and power to choose to see his situation as a lesson to learn, grow, and become stronger. To receive it as a test, a challenge. As an opportunity to overcome adversity. And, he would also be justified in that response. The choice is totally his.

Only you get to decide on your own attitudes, mindset, and responses. And, here is the kicker, however you decide to choose, you are justified in that choice. And, you will receive the corresponding consequences of your choice.

If you choose to feel like a victim, then you are, and you are justified. If you choose to feel like a victor, then you are a victor, and you are also justified in that choice. And in both cases, regardless of the choice, you will realize the effect and corresponding consequence of that choice.

In the hypothetical "John" example just presented, most people would quickly label his situation as "Bad", as a tragedy. But now we know that this label is just a choice we make and not a mandatory response. Depending on the specific choice it can serve the purpose causing one to feel destroyed, and despondent. Or grateful, hopeful, and victorious.

John has the power and right to choose to see his situation as a tragedy, or as an opportunity for transformation. If he chooses to see it as an opportunity, that is exactly what the situation becomes. An opportunity for finding inner strength, wisdom, deeper meaning and a positive, empowering outcome. You have the power to choose. This is a wonderfully liberating and empowering realization.

***"Everything can be taken from a man but one thing:
the last of human freedoms,
to choose one's attitude
in any given set of circumstances,
to choose one's own way"***
Victor E. Frankl

Through your choosing you can turn ANY situation from a problem into an opportunity. You can choose to receive anything that comes your way in this life in the perspective that most benefits you. This is your POWER. This is your right. This is how you can shape your circumstances, by choosing your perspective and responses. Your choices are completely yours to make and no one else's. Choosing and deciding for yourself is your ultimate, sovereign right. Choosing is unavoidable...and if you think that you can get out of it by not choosing…guess what? That is still a choice.

"If you choose not to decide,
you still have made a choice"
Neil Peart

Remember that every situation in life is simply presented to you as a cup filled ½ way… Is it half empty, or half full? Both are correct, but each perspective is significantly different in the effect it will have on your outlook, response, and outcome. The same situation can be viewed in significantly different ways and the effect and outcome will be shaped by that choice.

You see, the situations and circumstances we experience in life happen around us, near us, beside us, in front of us, etc. They happen outside of us. But, nothing happens IN us unless we choose it and accept it. Your life ultimately happens IN YOU. And you are the only one with the sovereign power to decide what it is that happens IN YOU.

"What happens TO you is not nearly as important
as what happens IN you."

Choose to label "Problems" as "Opportunities

Why choose to label something as a problem? Isn't it more empowering and just as true to label them as opportunities?

"The Problem is not the problem.
The problem is your attitude about the problem"

One thing you can be certain of in this life is that there will ALWAYS be situations that we will tend to label as problems, challenges, adversities, etc. Since you know this to be true, you should NOT be surprised, upset, or discouraged when they show up. What you MUST do is change your natural, disempowered tendency to label them as problems, frustrations, difficulties, etc. Instead choose to see them as they truly are.... OPPORTUNITIES!!!! Opportunities for understanding, growing, overcoming, learning, strengthening, for winning!!!!

"Every adversity carries with it
the seed of an equivalent benefit"
Napoleon Hill

Continually remind yourself that EVERY situation is there for your benefit. They present real opportunities for you to learn, understand and grow. That is why they are there. That is specifically why those situations have come to you. They have been personalized and tailor made for you because you need them to grow, to become wiser and to get better. Yes, you need those experiences. They are necessary for you.

This is where the words of the great stoic philosopher Marcus Aurelius can come to our aid. He wrote:

> ***"Our actions may be impeded, but there can be no impeding our intentions or dispositions. Because we can accommodate and adapt. The mind adapts and converts to its own purposes the obstacle to our acting. The impediment to action advances action. What stands in the way becomes the way"***

We must embrace the wonderful wisdom that is contained in this highly practical truth. That those very things that stand in our way, that we perceive as "obstacles" are really the path by which we must now travel. They contain the necessary lessons that prepare and enable us to reach our intended destination or outcome.

The obstacle in the way has now become the way. This problem that stands before me is the puzzle I must now solve to get me to the next level. That is why it is here. The fact that it is here, is a clear indication that I need it. I need to face it and to overcome it, in order for me to advance.

This obstacle that stands before me is NOT my enemy. I must accept and embrace it. I will not resist or reject it. It is not my foe, it is my necessary friend and ENABLER.

The empowered You avoids the obvious negative interpretations and labels. Because you know that when you label something as a problem, that is what it becomes, a problem. And it will yield for you all the consequences of this disempowering label. However, when you CHOOSE to see it as an opportunity, that is now what it becomes, an OPPORTUNITY. And this promises to yield for you the benefits that opportunities bring.

So, choose to see all the challenges that come your way as GOLDEN OPPORTUNITIES. Specifically designed for you to learn and GROW. Because you know that once you make that intentional and empowered choice, that is exactly what they become. Golden opportunities designed and delivered specifically for YOUR benefit.

Life is not out to get you.
It is looking out for you.

Life is not happening at you.
It is happening for you.

The Law of Laws...Cause and Effect

You see, the only inherent, intrinsic meaning in the things that happen, is that they happened for a reason. All things happen because something has caused it to happen. That is the reason. This is obvious and fundamental as it is settled by the Law of Cause and Effect. This law is inescapable and it states that every effect has a cause, and every cause has its corresponding effect.

All of life is ruled by this law, which Ralph Waldo Emerson called the "The Law of Laws". Since all that happens is determined by this law, we must therefore expose and expunge the disempowering concept called "chance". So, follow along, since we know that all the things that happen have a cause, then, clearly, there is nothing that happens "by chance".

Chance is NEVER the cause of anything!!!

Chance is simply the term we use to label things that we do not understand or cannot explain its cause. This concept of "chance" is a "no thing". It is meaningless, describes nothing, has NO power, and therefore it can cause NOTHING.

We only use the term "chance" when we are ignorant of the cause of a particular effect. Or when it is outside our ability to know or understand the actual cause of any specific effect.

A perfect example of this is what happens when you roll dice. You would typically say that you rolled the specific numbers that came up "by chance". But, it is not by chance that the dice rolled in that specific way. Because the dice must behave consistent with predictable physical laws. If you knew the precise position of the dice, the exact trajectory and force of the roll, the friction, the angle of bounce, etc., etc. Then you would be able to calculate and know exactly how the dice would end up. This would not be a mystery as every factor of rolling the dice is knowable and predictable.

The problem is that we don't have the ability to calculate all those factors. Because there is an overwhelming amount of data that we would have to consider, determine, and calculate. But those factors are all knowable and they have predictable results. As they are all subject to the law of cause and effect. But, since we do not have the capacity to calculate or know all those factors, we conveniently say that we rolled those specific numbers "by chance".

Chance is the term we use when we do not know the specific cause of an effect. So, we say it happened by "chance" out of our own ignorance. There is no such thing as chance…only cause and effect. Do you see this now? By the way, this also applies to the concept of "coincidence". Coincidence is another useless term that has no power and causes nothing. Nothing happens by coincidence. There is only cause and effect.

So, now that we have eliminated the deceptive and disempowering concepts of "chance" and "coincidence" we know that the only objective meaning that every situation brings with it, is that it has a specific cause. And in most cases the causes are obvious, since we can trace any and every effect back to its specific and direct cause. Because the law of cause and effect is always at work. It cannot be avoided or suspended. You cannot have an effect without a cause, or a cause without an effect.

Reason and Purpose

So now let's move forward to the next inevitable ramification of this cause/effect understanding. Let's make an important distinction between the words "reason" and "purpose". These two words can be synonymous but, there is an important nuance between them that is helpful to understand.

The meaning of the word reason is: "A cause, explanation, or justification for an action or event". The word "purpose" has a similar meaning, but it offers much more than that. As it points to something deeper and more profound.

Reason looks back, but purpose looks forward. The reason is the cause or explanation for the specific thing happening. Whereas, the purpose assigns the meaning to that thing or happening. Purpose points us forward to a yet to be realized outcome or consequence. It speaks to the future potential of the things that happen rather than simply to their cause.

The reason lies in the past, the purpose lies in the future. Can you see this important difference? The reason we cannot choose, as it is settled in the past. But the purpose is ours to choose. And that determines our future course.
Here are some simple examples of Reason versus Purpose.......

> The glass fell off the table.
> *The reason:* I accidently knocked it over.
> *The purpose*: I am reminded to be more careful.
>
> My wife got upset.
> *The reason:* I said something hurtful to her.
> *The purpose*: It reminds me to be more sensitive.
> To not say things that I know will upset her.

While these examples are very simple, the concept and distinction are powerful and can be applied to EVERY situation you experience.

You often hear people say, “everything happens for a reason” as if they are offering up some deep wisdom. But now we know that, of course, it’s obvious, everything happens for a reason. This is settled by the law of cause and effect. There was a reason it happened, as the reason is what caused it to happen. There is no question about this.

The real question is; What is the purpose for this thing happening? And it is YOU that gets to assign meaning and purpose to everything that happens in YOUR life. Because you understand and accept that life is not happening at you, but that life is happening for you. And therefore, everything that happens is intended to have a positive and meaningful purpose for you.

You get to choose and decide on the meaning and purpose for all the things that happen to you

Remember that every situation comes to us bearing ONLY the objective, obvious significance of its cause. That’s It!!! But the MEANING and PURPOSE it has in YOUR life is for YOU to determine. You get to determine the “going forward” by your own purposeful choosing. So, in everything you should ask; “How does this instruct, influence, and inspire me to move forward in an empowered and positive way?” And YOU get to determine the answer to these questions.

You can choose how you receive and respond to EVERYTHING that happens. This is where your POWER lies. And this power is yours alone for YOU. This is a KEY component of the POWER of Choosing.

Do you see it more clearly now? In this life YOU choose. Your responses, attitudes, actions, beliefs, goals, desires, hopes, dreams, aspirations, what you wear, eat, who you date, marry, love, where you go, what you do, etc. Choosing is your sovereign right, and in properly exercising that right you find your true POWER.

I encourage you to choose to see a positive purpose in every "problem" and an opportunity in every "obstacle". Ask yourself these questions when you are faced with a challenging situation:

Will this serve to break me down? Or BUILD ME UP?

Will this cause me to stop? Or KEEP ON GOING?

Is this a defeat? Or a step closer to my inevitable VICTORY?

Is this a problem? Or an OPPORTUNITY for me to grow and get better?

Will I serve this situation? Or will this situation serve ME?

Will this situation have power over me? Or will it EMPOWER me?

I am not telling you **WHAT** to choose.
I am only telling you **THAT** you choose.

It is your RIGHT to choose and, in that right, lies your POWER. Even if there are limited choices in any situation, you still have an infinite ability to determine how to receive and benefit from those limited choices. Make the best of it or the worst of it, or somewhere in between…You Choose.

Some choices and decisions carry little consequence, some greater. The starting point is for you to be keenly aware that in life, you choose. With this understanding, you can then decide to be more aware of your choosing.

To properly wield the power of choosing in an empowered way you must become a more conscious and intentional chooser. This is KEY. Here is the simple 3 step process to becoming a more conscious, intentional, and empowered chooser.

Step #1: Be present.
Focus on right here, right now.

Step #2: Be intentional and purposeful.
What outcome do you desire? Be honest and clear.

Step #3: Simply CHOOSE,
Consistent with your conscious intentions. Then, make an Empowered Decision (see the "Be Decisive" Habit)

The following two EMPOWERMENT HABITS will enable you to become a more Empowered chooser.

Empowerment Habit:

Be Present

"Wherever you are, be there. If you can be fully present now, you'll know what it means to live."
Steve Goodier

I AM… Present. I actively practice being in the moment. Because In this very moment is where my peace and my power lie. I know the only time I can affect any change is in the here and now.

In order to become a more "conscious chooser" you must train yourself to continually practice setting your attention and intentions in the HERE & NOW. This can be a challenging discipline but, as with any practice, it gets easier the more you do it. I challenge you to commit to making this a key habit in your life.

We must be reminded that life is a succession of nows. There is no yesterday, no tomorrow…only now. We must become practiced in the art of living in the moment. It is only in the now where you can find you already possess all you truly need. Because it is only ever the present moment that holds the promise of your happiness and fulfillment. It is only in the right here, right now that you can choose your attitude and mindset.

In this very moment, you can choose to discover that you are complete and content. You do not need anything else other than to embrace this very moment and receive the peace and fulfillment it contains. Regardless of any outside circumstance.

Our power always and only ever lies in the present moment. The only time we can do anything is right here, right now. To become a more conscious and intentional chooser you must, therefore, practice being present. Being in the moment. Because the only time you can affect any change or establish any control over your life is right here and now….in the moment.

"The best time to have planted a tree was twenty years ago. The second-best time is now."

Sadly, most of us are too preoccupied with yesterday, or what happened this morning, or worrying about what tomorrow will bring, It is hard for our thoughts and emotions to be right here, right now. In the present moment.

"We live regretful of yesterday, fearful of tomorrow, and forgetful of right now"

We must redirect our tendency to be regretful of the past, anxious about the future and forgetful of the present. And, instead, we must choose to BE:

Grateful for the past

Hopeful about the future

Mindful of the present.

It is only when we are thinking of the past or the future that we tend to experience doubt, worry, and anxiety. In the here and now there is no worry, doubt, or fear. Only peace and contentment, if you choose it. Choose to live from the inside out, in the moment.

***"If you are depressed, you are living in the past.
If you are anxious, you are living in the future.
If you are at peace, you are living in the moment"***
Lao Tzu

Living in the moment is also called mindfulness. This is the state where you are intentional and focused on the present moment. To quiet what the Buddhists call our "Monkey Mind". They call it that because our minds have the tendency to be constantly jumping around from one branch of thought to another.

However, when you practice mindfulness, you can step outside of your thoughts and realize that you are NOT your thoughts, but rather, the observer of your thoughts. And thus, you can then better direct and determine the flow and content of your thoughts. Becoming more present in your thinking and perspective. Be more mindful.

***"Yesterday is history,
Tomorrow is a mystery,
but the present is a gift.
This is why it is called
the present."***

Empowerment Habit:

Be Decisive

"Decisions Determine Destiny"

I AM… Decisive. I make empowered decisions that are definitive and binding. These empowered decisions chart the course of my empowered life.

Remember that we have a physical, mental, and emotional tendency to stay the same. Because the pull of precedent and the law of inertia are constantly at work in our lives pressing upon us. Causing us to keep repeating the same predictable, "comfortable" patterns.

It is your decision making that provides an effective force that enables you to break the hold of inertia that is causing you to stay in the ruts created by your subconscious, unintentional, disempowering conditioning. You must be practiced at making effective decisions. Because it is in your deciding that there exists the power to break your tendency to stay the same.

Your deciding must be that greater force that enables you to move in a new, and different direction. A direction that is consistent with your intentional desires, hopes, and goals.

Before I explain empowered decision making, you must first understand the full and true meaning of the word "decision". Because understanding what the word truly means will prove to be extremely helpful in enabling you to make the proper application of this process called deciding.

Word Study

The word "**Decision**" comes from the Latin verb "**Caedo**".
Which means **"to cut or to kill".**

From this Latin verb, we also get the words:
"Incision" and "**Precision".**

"Incision" means, to **CUT into**.

"Precision" means, to **CUT beforehand**.
As in a very thoughtful and premeditated way.
Hence the prefix "Pre".

"Decision" means, a **CUTTING away from**.

Thus, in keeping with the true meaning of the word, a decision is meant to be a definite cutting away of all other possible options, or outcomes. When you decide, you are supposed to cut away all other options. And, in the process of "cutting off" those other possible options, you also effectively kill them off. Yes, the other options are supposed to be dead as the result of your cutting them off by your deciding. This is the true meaning and intent of the word.

Notice that the word "decide" uses the same form of the Latin verb that is used in the words homicide, suicide, infanticide, patricide, etc. Because it follows that once you decide, you have cut off and at the same time, effectively "killed off" the other options.

So, you see, decision making is intended to be a forceful, and definitive act. When you decide, you pick ONE outcome, ONE option. And, in the process, you effectively cut away and "kill off" all the other possibilities. The other possibilities should NO LONGER EXIST for you. Because they are now dead and lifeless, since you have cut them off and away.

Understanding and applying the true and proper meaning of deciding is key to living an empowered life. Because you now understand that to decide is to perform a very deliberate and definitive act. Where you no longer give ANY consideration to the alternatives. Because they have been cut away and eliminated. They no longer exist.

Empowered decision making is a two-part process

#1. Make the decision that you desire.

Cutting away the other available possibilities, options, or potential outcomes.

#2. Do NOT entertain the "cut off" options.

Since you have effectively cut away and killed the other options, they must remain dead and therefore powerless over you. They have been cut away. They are DEAD!!! They are NOT to be entertained or considered any further. As doing so will detract you from your decision.

In order for the "cut away" options to remain DEAD and powerless, they must not be given any further consideration. You must not give them ANY life in your thinking. DO not allow any thought to enter your mind that will distract or dissuade you from the initial decision or choice that you have intentionally made.

This is a KEY discipline in developing self-mastery. Because you know that anything you entertain in your mind will grow in its power of influence over you. So, once you have decided, you must keep the door SHUT, not allowing any consideration to the dead alternatives.

Once you have decided on a course of action it is normal for your mind to surface thoughts of the alternative decisions or options. It is normal to second guess and, to some degree, think about the alternatives. This tendency, if unchecked, will create a double mindedness that will only serve to disempower you. You must exercise the discipline to keep those things cut away. Not doing so will distract you from your stated goal or objective.

True, empowered decision making must involve this two-fold process. You decide what you want, and simultaneously determine NOT to allow any distracting thought or temptation to enter your consideration. You are NOT to entertain the "dead" alternatives that you have cut away by your intentional and purposeful decision.

Being decisive means becoming single minded. Not close minded, but single minded. There is a difference. You must be open minded when considering your options. However, once you decide, the door is SHUT to the alternatives, and therefore you can now set out to achieve and accomplish. To realize your decisions. The single-minded person will accomplish what they set out to obtain. However, the timid, double minded person will fail before they even begin.

"If you chase two rabbits,
you will not catch either one"
Proverb

As an example, if you have decided to not eat meat for health or other reasons, the minute you find yourself getting carried away by the thought of a juicy steak, you must STOP and cut that thought away. Remembering that you made an intentional decision and part of that decision was to NOT give ANY consideration to thoughts of the alternatives that can sway you from your intentional decision. The other options MUST remain dead and hence, powerless over you. They are no longer in consideration, they must not and should not be resurrected in your mind.

This mental practice of proper decision making is very powerful. And, you can apply it to every decision that you make. From the little to the big things. True empowered decision making is very powerful and highly effective.

The Beach Story

Let me share a personal example that while very simple, I believe clearly illustrates how we can become more effective when we understand and apply proper empowered decision making to both the little and big things in our lives.

I was at the beach with my family one Sunday morning. It was a beautiful sunny day, but it was spring time, so the ocean water was still quite cold. This fact was obvious because while there were many people enjoying the sand and sun, very few were in the ocean.

Upon arriving and setting up our chairs and umbrellas; I determined that I would not be going in the water. That I would sit in the beach chair, relax, read, and watch my children play in the sand. However, about an hour later my daughter said she wanted to go in the water and asked her brother to go in with her. He promptly protested, saying that he did not want to. So, not wanting to disappoint my daughter, I decided that I would go in the water with her. Right away and without ANY hesitation, I promptly stood up, took off my shirt, made my way straight up to the water and dove in. My only thought during that time was "I am getting in the water".

I made a clear decision and acted on it by not considering any of the other factors that I would normally entertain when making this decision. Factors like, being self-conscious of taking off my shirt in public, or that the water was very cold, etc. Factors that would potentially dissuade me from my decision to get in the water. This time I was single-mindedly focused on my decision to get in the water, period!

When I tell this story, people often ask “and you did not feel how cold that water was, right?”. No, I did feel that the water was VERY cold, but that did not matter. What mattered was that I made the decision to get in the water and that was the only thing I focused and acted on. I was single-minded and did NOT entertain any other consideration that would dissuade me from my decision. My only thought was, “get in the water”.

I was struck by this little exercise in proper, forceful, decision making. Which, by the way, is how I now decide to go in the water whenever I go to the beach. I stand straight up, take off my shirt, walk directly to the water and dive right in…No hesitation, just a single-minded decision to “get in the water”.

It was amusing to watch how other people made their “decision” to get in the water. How they would first dip their toe, then slowly make their way in. The startled look in their faces as they experienced the cold water. The slow agonizing way that they would eventually get in the water. Some would even scurry back out before getting all the way in, immediately regretting their decision to go in the water.

This scene served as an accurate visual representation of how many people make “decisions” in their lives. The “dip their toes”, they focus more on the temperature of the water rather than their decision to get in the water. I say if you decide to get in the water, then just DO IT…Get IN the water.

This simple example can serve as an effective model for making the same type of empowered decisions in other areas of our lives. When you decide, it is intended to be a single-minded act where in the process of your deciding you also determine to IGNORE any alternatives that will only serve to distract or dissuade you from your decision.

Empowered Decisions

Making empowered decisions becomes the way that you move forward in your life. If there are things that you are not happy or satisfied with, then it calls for you to make an empowered decision that will enable you to move in a different direction. Breaking the hold of inertia and getting you out of your comfort zones to experience the better and different things you truly desire.

If you decide to get up early to start an exercise regime or a special project, then you will get up early. If you decide to stop eating certain foods, because you want to lose weight or develop a healthier diet then do so. If you decide to marry someone, you do so and then continually decide to stay in that relationship and make it work as you stay faithful to that decision. Because it is your intention to do so and you will inevitably always move in the direction of your stated intentions.

Even if you are not mentally ready to make an important empowered decision in some area of your life, at least now you are aware of this process. And this will already set up your intentionality and your subconscious mind will over time become your silent enabler. As you have set up that mental paradigm of what an empowered decision is truly meant to be. When your want power is activated, you will decide and move forward.

Since we now understand how empowered decisions are to be made, we do not make them lightly. When we make them, we know they are to be binding and definitive. We do not look to the right or to the left, but straight ahead along the path of our deciding. Knowing that any of the possible distractions or temptations are simply no longer in our consideration.

Therefore, you need to be convinced that a decision needs to be made and that you are clear and convinced about your decision. If you are not certain and clear, then you must set your intentionality on guiding you towards being certain of what decision you should make.

So, step one is to get to the place where you can see clearly and be certain of the decision you want to make with a view to the next step that once decided on it is definitive. Always remembering that a truly empowered decision is one that is immediately followed up by the decision to not allow any distracting thought or competing consideration. Where you say, "I will not entertain anything that will distract me or influence to disempower me from staying in my intentional decision".

Do not make decisions where you find yourself resisting to stay in that decision. Because it should not be about resisting, but a determined cutting away of the alternatives. Resistance is futile, because you will likely give in. But a cutting away is FINAL.

Why is this important? Because we have a tendency towards second guessing our decisions. The minute we make a choice, thoughts will tend to surface that will question that choice. Or we question our ability or likelihood of achieving that goal. When deciding and choosing we must be forceful and definitive.

The act of true deciding is an effective use of your conscious intention that sets you in a definite, desired direction. You have the POWER to choose and then to decide, but you must make your decisions powerful and effective. Empowered decisions provide us the FORCE needed in order to break the hold of inertia and sameness that keeps us in the quicksand of our discontent.

Now that you understand the true meaning of deciding, as you examine how most people go about making decisions, you may find that, in most cases, they are not really deciding at all. As it is not true and effective decision making but, instead, a soft form of choosing that is often quickly ignored and abandoned. Proving that it was never a real decision in the true sense of the word. Like deciding to "get in the water" but quickly becoming diverted or discouraged and not getting in all the way, or at all.

Understanding the true meaning of the word will empower you to make true decisions that have the power to cause effective change in your lives. However, as you persevere to apply this new understanding of proper decision making you need to be aware that there is quite often something else very powerful at work in you that may often limit or hamper your full ability to choose.

Subconscious Programming

The reality of our choice making is a bit more complex, as there are other factors that come into play that we may not always be consciously aware of. As I will further discuss in the following section on the conscious and subconscious mind, we all have an innate and exceptional ability to "automate" processes.

While this is a very useful ability, it is also true that this can often serve us in negative and dis-empowering ways. As we may find that in many situations we may be operating, not from our present conscious intentions and purposes, but from prior conditioning and subconscious programming. And it is this disempowering condition of operating from prior programming that often predetermines what responses, attitudes, or actions we will tend to automatically choose.

We have all developed automatic response programs in our thinking, feeling, and acting that are deeply ingrained in our subconscious mind. Once these responses are "triggered" we automatically run that program without being consciously aware of why we are reacting or choosing as we do.

As such, we are not always able to simply make choices that are totally intentional, unbiased, or without "baggage". Choices that reflect our true wants and desires. Because, sadly, we often respond out of these pre-conditioned, subconscious responses that bypass our true intentions by shortcutting our conscious mind.

It is our very own subconscious programming that can potentially rob us of our ability to make intentional, empowered choices. As in many situations, we no longer consider the options, instead we become “triggered” and simply run the most ingrained program without our conscious awareness. And many of these pre-programmed subconscious responses may be working against us. They may be preventing us from choosing consistent with who we want to be, or from feeling how we truly want to feel. They often take us hostage in a direction that is contrary to our true wants, desires, and intentions.

Subconscious Trigger in the Attic

Let me share a powerful, personal example of a preprogrammed physical automatic response. When I was younger, I installed home burglar alarm systems. This was the time before wireless systems. So, to install an alarm system, you had to run wires that would connect the sensors from each opening of the house back to the control panel and keypad. That work involved having to crawl around the hot attic of the house in order to install the wiring. While doing the attic crawling I would sweat profusely. Inevitably, my glasses would slip down the bridge of my nose and I would have to repeatedly nudge them back up to prevent them from falling off.

I did this type of alarm installation work for several years but eventually sold the business. About a year or so after selling the business, as a favor to a friend, I agreed to install his alarm system. At that time, I no longer wore glasses. But, as I was in the process of crawling in the attic installing the wiring, all the sudden, I nudged my “glasses” back up the bridge of my nose.

The interesting thing is that I was NOT wearing glasses. I was amused by what I had just done since I had not worn glasses for about a year. Yet here I was automatically repeating a response triggered by that external situation. And the real scary part was that after having done it once, and catching myself, a few minutes later, I did it AGAIN. This showed me in a very profound way, how powerful subconscious programming can be.

The realization that I would perform a specific physical act without needing to do it, and without consciously initiating it. Simply because somehow, I had been subconsciously programmed to do it, was very concerning.

I realized that I had caught myself running a very deeply ingrained, conditioned, pre-programmed response…Like Pavlov's dogs. I had experienced a preprogrammed automatic response that was triggered by a specific external condition.

At that moment, I was "triggered" to act in a specific way without thinking or consciously choosing. I did something that totally bypassed my conscious intention. Something I did not want to do, had no need to do, or any reason to do it. Yet I did it anyway. Without a conscious thought. And not only once, but twice!!! This experience both, intrigued, and concerned me.

This was a significant realization because I knew it carried deep implications and potential consequences in my life. How many other subconscious programs have been ingrained in me? That are "choosing" my actions during different situations and set off by certain triggers? And not just my physical actions, but emotional responses, and patterns of thinking also.

This is a KEY question that we must continually ask and determine about ourselves. In the process of your empowerment you must identify and untangle yourself from any preprogrammed response that may be limiting and disempowering you.

How often do you do things "automatically" without having an intention, need, desire, or reason to do it? Think about this. Be honest. How often do you act in irrational or unintentional ways? How often do you ask ourselves, "why did I do that silly or stupid thing? Why did I say that? Why do I react this way? Why do I find myself feeling a certain way that I do not want to feel? Why do I always get into this negative mindset when this thing happens, or when a certain person treats me a certain way, or when I am in a certain situation, Etc…."

We all have deeply pre-programmed physical, emotional, and thought responses in all areas of our lives. The reason for this is because once you respond to something a certain way, you set a precedent, and now a subconscious pattern starts to form. If we are not guarded, intentional, and self-aware, the pattern can take hold and become a subconscious automatic response that simply needs a trigger to set it in motion. It now becomes an automatic response that no longer needs the approval of your conscious mind. It effectively slips past your conscious filter. Scary, right?

Accompanying our preprogrammed responses are the triggers that set them off. We all have certain situations that act like triggers causing us to mindlessly run an accompanying pre-programmed response.

So how can we deal with this in an empowered way? We must be HIGHLY SELF AWARE and catch these as they happen. Then, we must make conscious choices as to whether we want to continue allowing those pre-programmed responses to run and affect our lives. Or, we can decide that they do not serve us in positive ways and that we want to change them.

To effect change in your pre-programmed responses you must practice being **present, purposeful, and intentional**. Not robotic and mindlessly running programs of preconditioned actions or triggered responses. You have no effective power when acting in these ways. You have power when you act with purpose and intention. The more intentional you are, the more powerful you are. See empowerment Rule #7: Your intentionality determines your potentiality.

It is an important realization to understand that whenever you do, say, feel, or think things that you did not want to, need to, or have a reason to. It is likely because of subconscious conditioned programming that you have developed.

This realization is KEY in helping you to expose unwanted and disempowering pre-programmed responses that manifest not only in your physical actions, but also in your emotions and patterns of thought. You must become more SELF AWARE.

When you think, feel, or act in ways that you did not necessarily want to or need to, it is because you are running preprogrammed, triggered, conditioned, subconscious responses.

What is the cure for these unintentional preprogrammed responses?

Step one: Become aware of what is happening. You must be more self-aware. Once you become aware of, and understand that you are running a preprogrammed, limiting, or defeating response, it has now become exposed. Once exposed, it's power over you is immediately diminished. And you can, over time, begin to consciously and intentionally create a new way of thinking, feeling, and reacting. One of your intentional, purposeful choosing.

Do not get married to your responses. Always maintain some level of distance so you can look at them more objectively. This way you can determine if they serve a positive or a disempowering purpose. Your reactions and responses are not necessarily "you". So, do not feel like you must protect and defend them. Especially when they are not benefitting you or others. They may be in need of re-directing or changing altogether.

Step two: Be present and intentional. This way you can consciously decide that you want to take a different approach. That you want to have a different attitude, a different way of thinking, feeling, speaking, acting. The change will not happen overnight, but it WILL happen over time. Remember, you are in control, and through your present and intentional conscious thoughts and actions you can, over time change any behaviors that you determine to change.

You must have this confidence because it is true that, ultimately, YOU are in charge of YOU. Your subconscious programming is not your enemy. Your subconscious is only trying to be helpful. It is only running the programs it believes you want to run because you have run them in the past or indulged them in the past. You can change if you choose. And you do this by becoming more mindful, conscious, and consistent in your intentions. You can thus develop new subconscious patterns that are more empowering and productive.

When you catch yourself in a pre-programmed state, remind yourself that this is not the conscious "you" doing this. That it is an automatic preprogrammed response that somehow you have been conditioned to run. It is important for you to expose this and assert, if you choose, that this is NOT what you want. Declare that you no longer want this response to take hold of you. This declaration of your true intention is a key step in breaking the pre-programmed pattern.

Understanding why you have been conditioned to run this response is also helpful in undoing it, but it is not necessary. What is key, is that you are consciously aware that how you are responding, or feeling is a conditioned response. And that you determine to set your intentionality towards wanting to change this pattern.

Take mental notes of situations when you find yourself in a state of mind or acting in ways that do not serve your intentional desires. It may be helpful to write down the specifics of the situations. How you felt, the circumstance, and what you think may have caused the automatic response. Also, note why you feel this response or attitude is counterproductive to your true goals and intentions. As you take time to think about it, you will gain a new level of understanding and awareness. This form of intentional self-analysis is powerful and will imitate the process of change that you desire.

Writing down your insights is an effective way of self-analyzing. It will help enable you to better direct the power of your conscious intentions thereby allowing you to best determine the new subconscious programming that you will allow to become ingrained in you. As you do so, you will find that when you fall into those situations in the future, you will be more self-aware. You will then have more conscious power over the situation and can start to change those negative disempowering responses and develop new patterns of your intentional choosing.

You need to expose the programmed behavior or emotion that you want to change. Then insert new programming. When certain patterns or outside triggers occur, you can decide what new principles or beliefs you want to "insert here"? Once you feed your subconscious mind a specific and desired new principle or paradigm it will accept it and eventually respond in congruence with it.

You will start creating more intentional programming consistent with your empowerment mindset and beliefs. Do not become frustrated or upset if the change is not immediate because in most cases it will not be. But take comfort in the fact that you are now more conscious and aware, and this will sow the seeds of change that will cause the new programming to start developing.

State to yourself… "I will not let the outside situation determine my inside feelings, etc.…I will not allow this person to cause me to get angry, fearful etc.…. this is just a test for me to learn grow…. etc.…." This type of "self-talk" will now start influencing the new programming that is being impressed upon your subconscious mind. Over time it will accept it and act on it more and more. It must, as this is what it was designed to do. So be confident and patient and persistent.

Don't let life push your buttons. Be more mindful and self-aware, because in that state you can DECIDE what responses, emotions, and attitudes will best serve YOU in every situation.

Be more aware of preprogrammed responses when dealing with work situations or in your personal relations. How are you reacting to your wife, kids, relatives, etc.? How are you reacting when certain issues come up at work? Are your reactions and choices driven by your conscious, intentional choosing, or are you being swept away by prior conditioning into feelings, emotions, words, or actions that do not produce positive outcomes for you or those around you?

Are you reacting to people and situations, or intentionally choosing your responses? Are you being "triggered" and responding in ways you do not need to, or desire? Or are you consciously and intentionally choosing your mindset and responses?

Be mindful of any pre-programmed attitudes and responses you may have unconsciously allowed yourself to develop. As you will likely find that many are not serving you in a positive or empowering way. That they are in fact limiting you and proving to be hurtful to your relationships, work life, and emotional well-being.

"Habit took the advantage of inattention; inclination was sometimes too strong for reason"
Ben Franklin

It is only when we have a lack of attention or purposeful reasoning that habit can spring up and take us away in an unwanted direction. If you find yourself taking a negative or disempowering attitude or response, catch and correct yourself. Be aware and call it out as something you do NOT want.

Even if you are not sure how to change your current emotion or attitude. That's ok, just be certain as you assert that you do NOT want it. Because it all starts with your intentionality. Set your intentionality to choose to want to break that negative pattern of thinking, feeling, or acting.

Ask yourself, "Going forward, how do I want this situation to play out in my mind. How do I want to respond to my wife when this happens? At work this thing happened, how can I see it as a positive?

By setting your intentionality you will start to break any negative patterns that may have unconsciously formed over time. Again, it will not happen overnight, but you must trust that it will happen over time.

"You are not in charge of the universe,
but you are in charge of yourself"
Arnold Bennet

Ask yourself, why do I think that I am doing this? What is causing this in me? As you ask these questions you are directing your conscious mind to surface the answers, and this will help you become more self-aware. Once the answers come then you can deal with them in a conscious and intentional way. This process of self-analyzing through self-awareness will become a powerful tool for you towards displaying more of your Empowered Self.

In the process, it is important not to beat yourself up or judge yourself. Do not be your own worst enemy. Forgive yourself and then simply set and declare to yourself your desired intentionality. Realize that it is an opportunity and accept it as such. Be patient with yourself as changing any process takes time. This will start the powerful process of change as you will over time, inevitably realize whatever it is that you purposely and persistently declare and desire for yourself.

Being present and intentional are the keys to empowered choosing. Right here right now, what do I really want? What is my truest and deepest intention and desire? You must choose consistent with your true wants and desires. Choosing your actions, attitudes, emotions, goals, desires, etc. This takes practice, conscious awareness….and TIME.

You will become more intentional and powerful in directing and making your life and habit choices. This will influence your thinking, attitude, emotions, and your resulting actions and outcomes. We must remember that when we act in purposeful and intentional ways, we are god like. However, when we act in preprogrammed conditioned ways, we are animal like.

You must continually remind yourself that you have the power to choose your responses in any and every situation. You decide what to say, think, or do when faced with any situation. You must be aware of and determine the conscious responses that are consistent with your true choosing rather than running pre-programmed responses. Be conscious of what state of mind you choose to take. Choose positive, constructive mindsets and responses.

In every situation, you must take a positive and empowering approach. Resisting the negative mindsets or negative self-talk. Refuse to say to yourself "I am frustrated, I am defeated, etc.". As this will color your mindset and incline you towards those feelings. Even if you are feeling frustrated, keep in mind this IMPORTANT fact: The emotions that your subconscious mind is offering up are only suggestions. It should be your conscious mind that ultimately decides what emotions, mindsets, actions are desirable and consistent with your intentional desires. Because after all you are NOT "frustrated, upset, defeated", etc. That is NOT who you are, those are simply emotions that you have somehow allowed yourself to experience. And you have the power to choose differently.

The quality of our lives is based on the quality of our choices and our choices are all mental determinations. These mental determinations then result in your feelings, your actions….and ultimately, your outcomes.

To become more empowered and to realize a more positive and productive life, you must always remember that every situation you encounter is there to serve you.

Life is not happening at you it is happening for you. Simply choose to see the challenges, problems, and frustrations that come into your life as the opportunities that they really are. Opportunities for you to have victory over them. They are there to serve YOU. For you to grow and become stronger, better, wiser.

Every situation is either your teacher, or your master. In every trial, you will either become better or bitter, a victim or victorious. You choose, and whatever you choose will become true for you, as you will be justified in that choice and will realize the corresponding outcome of that choice.

When choosing from the empowered perspective you will not only grow and become more confident and fulfilled, but you will also benefit and bless those around you. You will become a light of encouragement and a source of strength and hope for others who desperately need it.

When you begin to see all the circumstances in your life as having been purposely designed and delivered to you personally for the primary purpose of your growing, learning, and becoming more victorious, then you will live a TRANSFORMED, CONFIDENT and EMPOWERED life.

Receive all that happens with thanksgiving and humility. Be nonjudgmental and accepting of ALL of life's circumstances. Use them for the positive purposes of YOUR CHOOSING. Trust and know this is so. Embrace all that comes your way, because…you are BIGGER than your challenges and stronger that your difficulties. You are POWER-FULL...Not POWER-LESS…. Because you always have the POWER TO CHOOSE.

"Destiny is no matter of chance.
It is a matter of choice.
It is not a thing to be waited for,
it is a thing to be achieved."
William Jennings Bryan

INTERLUDE

Your Conscious & Subconscious Mind

In this section, we will pause to get a basic understanding of our marvelous and incredible mind. This information will be key to setting a foundation to properly explain and understand the remaining Empowerment Rules. So, sit back, get comfortable and let's go on a journey of the mind. (I always wanted to say that.)

While I believe that we are much more than our minds, it is safe to say that our mind is our primary tool, mechanism, and means by which we experience and realize our lives.

It is hard to overstate the importance of having a clearer understanding of our marvelous mind and how that relates to who we are or believe ourselves to be. And how this determines the quality of our lives. Let's face it, for the most part, **the quality of our thought life IS the quality of our lives.**

This information to follow on the conscious and subconscious mind is by no means exhaustive or clinical. And I encourage you to study this further if it is of interest to you. However, I trust that what we will cover in this chapter will prove to be very useful. Especially in the context of our message of EMPOWERMENT.

The mind is typically categorized as being composed of two "parts". The conscious and subconscious mind. There is a third part called the unconscious mind but, for our purposes, and so not to get overly complicated, we will attribute this part of the mind to our subconscious. So, we will simply focus on breaking it down to those two component parts. The Conscious and the Subconscious mind.

We are cognitive, perceptive, intuitive, deductive, emoting, sentient, self-aware, active beings. We exist and operate in an environment that has both physical and non-physical qualities.

List of functions/faculties attributed to our Conscious Mind:

Awareness of, and ability to process the sense perceptions.
Awareness of, and ability to direct stream of thoughts
Plan, rationalize, deduct, infer, compare, decide etc.
Pay attention and focus
Able to pull information from subconscious mind
Ability to train, to do something new
Imagine, visualize, pretend, day dream
Process details and make decisions
Organize, communicate, etc.

List of functions/faculties attributed to our subconscious mind:

Direct all bodily activities and functions (heart rate, breathing, digestion, etc.).
Generate emotions, feelings (based on thought or experience).
Storehouse for all Memories, Feelings, emotions, Beliefs
Direct base level awareness (wake up due to noise, pain, etc.)
Source of the stream of thoughts (not consciously directed)
Source of innate and instinctive behaviors
Source of stream of undirected visualization - daydream, dreams, etc.
Generates bodily feelings and emotions based on thoughts, as well as due to direct unconscious perceptions or habits.
Stores our memories and life experiences, not just the objective but also the subjective feelings.
It perfectly stores all memories from every sensory perception.

The conscious mind can only focus on a limited number of activities or processes at any one time. While the subconscious mind is virtually unlimited in the amount of information it can process. The subconscious mind has a seemingly inexhaustible amount of processing capability.

The subconscious mind directs all the ongoing activities of the trillions of cells in our body and does this effortlessly, without breaking a sweat or ever needing a rest or taking a day off. The subconscious mind never sleeps and is the storehouse of every memory, feeling, and experience we have EVER had as well as all the information we have EVER received. The power of the subconscious mind is incredible…it boggles the mind. No pun intended. The subconscious mind is the most super of all the super computers. More powerful than anything man has ever encountered or imagined.

It is important to point out that this incredible mind belongs to YOU. It is yours and intended as the means by which your body is kept alive. But more than that. It is also your primary tool that enables you to THRIVE. It is your primary tool to live, experience, act, and realize in this life.

Together, the conscious and subconscious comprise your ONE mind. This one mind is all yours. It knows you intimately and loves you. It wants the best for you and has the full capability to enable you to live the empowered life of your choosing. Yes, you are perfectly equipped to live an AMAZING and EMPOWERED life.

There is a wonderful and seamless interplay between both elements of our one mind. The conscious and subconscious. In order for us to realize our empowered self we must be aware of this wonderful relation, this interesting “marriage” of our one mind out of these two distinct faculties.

We have all the hardware we need to be AMAZING and EFFECTIVE. The problem is not the capability of our hardware. The problem is the quality and usefulness of the software and the programs we have loaded into our minds over time.

It is only to the degree that we can understand, order, and direct the mind that we will realize our goals, hopes, and desires in every area of our lives. Because, **the quality of our thinking determines the quality of our living.**

AUTOMATED ME

One critically important ability of our mind is the ability to automate physical, mental, and emotional processes or patterns. This ability is necessary. Primarily for the purposes of our routine life activities. If we did not possess this ability, we would always be consciously thinking about how to walk, eat, etc. Think about how important this ability is. How very useful and necessary it is for us to have quality of life.

Let's use the familiar experience of driving a car. To learn to drive a car you must apply your full conscious capacity to perform all the mechanical functions needed to control and direct the vehicle. When first learning to drive, it seems overwhelming and near impossible to perform all the different functions needed for proper control of the vehicle. But with repeated practice we find that driving becomes very easy to do. We can drive long distances in highway or city traffic and sometimes not even realize or be aware of how we got there. This once seemingly overwhelming conscious activity can now be almost totally performed by the subconscious mind. With little or no burden on the conscious mind.

At first, driving a car is an overwhelming experience, but with repeated practice it becomes as easy as drinking a glass of water. Same thing with riding a bike, playing an instrument, etc.…At first these functions seem difficult and overwhelming, but with conscious practice the entire complicated process can be performed by the subconscious mind in an easy, effortless way. (See Rule #9: It is Supposed to Be Easy).

This "automation" happens in all the basic daily functions that we perform. From the simple things like walking, brushing our teeth, putting on clothes. To performing more complex functions at work, in sports, etc....

This ability of our mind to learn a process initiated by the conscious mind, and then seamlessly "hand it over" to the subconscious paints a beautiful picture of the wonderful synergy and interplay between our conscious and subconscious mind. A lovely, faithful, practical, and efficient partnership between these two parts of our one mind.

The subconscious mind seems always ready, willing, and anxious to see what the conscious mind wants to do so that it can "take over" and automate that process or task. It is as if the subconscious mind is always saying "I am right here. Now that I know you want to do this, I can take care of it, "I got this". You can go and focus on other things."

Anything the conscious mind initiates as a physical, emotional, thought, or behavior pattern, the subconscious mind is willing and eager to take over. And it does it better, as you do not have to consciously think about it once it is taken over and automated by the subconscious mind, it just happens. With little or no need of your conscious attention. This is a wonderful (but potentially problematic) capability we all possess.

The subconscious mind continually unburdens the conscious mind because the conscious mind can only process and focus on a limited number of information/input at any one time. The subconscious mind is the enabler that allows the conscious mind to continually be freed up so that it can perform the critical functions that only it can perform.

The subconscious mind is a most willing and capable helper. It does not judge or discriminate it simply says to the conscious mind "Yes, I got this. Let me take care of this so you can do what only you are qualified to do on our behalf".

This ability we possess to automate a process is critical for us to effectively function in this life. However, as we discussed in the prior chapter, we can also create negative, limiting, and disempowering automated responses or patterns of feeling, thinking, and acting. If we are not mindful and self-aware, the automatic programming can become counterproductive and disempowering.

The subconscious mind is nonjudgmental. It does not question or argue with you. It simply accepts anything that is impressed upon it and simply goes with it. Any pattern that is continually allowed to run is reinforced and eventually automated by the subconscious mind. Good or bad, empowering or disempowering.

The subconscious mind is always on and always paying attention. It is recording everything and always respond by saying “YES”. The subconscious mind accepts everything, regardless of whether it is “real” or imagined.

The subconscious mind does NOT know the difference between something real and something you just imagine or think of.

To the subconscious mind there is no discerning. It is not bothered by the details of whether something is real (physical/visible) or imagined. This is the reason why when you are asleep, everything that you are dreaming of seems real to you at the time. It seems like it is really happening. And it is, it is happening in this altered state of being. You believe that what you are dreaming is actually happening. This is because it is your subconscious mind that is awake while the conscious mind “sleeps”. In the dream state, you believe that what is happening is real because it is your subconscious mind that is doing the processing. It is not until the conscious mind is awake that it now asserts and accepts that it was a dream and not “reality”.

The fact that the subconscious mind does not know the difference between something "real" and something imagined is NOT a limitation or a defect. Because, you see, the subconscious mind understands that we exist in a field of infinite potentiality (more on that later). It knows that anything we can imagine we can realize. Which is why it is not bothered by the incidental details regarding whether something exists in the physical, realized state, or in the potential state of infinite possibilities. It is not bound by the same limitations that we consciously place on our awareness and understanding. The subconscious mind is mysteriously plugged in to the universal field of potentiality. It knows that all possibilities exist, and if the possibility exists, then they can become realized, given the favorable means, resources, and conditions. It knows this instinctually. It is the conscious mind that places the limitations.

This is the reason that the subconscious mind only knows one word and that word is "YES". See Empowerment Rule #10: The Answer is "Yes".

It says "Yes" for two reasons; First, because it is your mind and will never argue with you. It will always accept what you impress upon it. Second, it says "yes" because it knows that all things exist in the state of potentiality and as such can be realized. It is not hung up by the senses or by the limitations that our senses can naturally impose on our conscious mind.

The subconscious mind will always say yes and then rationalize for you as it is your absolute best friend. It wants the best for you. It wants to protect you, but it does not discern (that is the job of your conscious mind).

If you tell yourself "I am a loser", your subconscious mind says "yes, you are" and it will find the reasons why this is true.

If you say, "This is horrible" it says "yes" and finds reasons why this is so.

If you say, "this is great", it says "yes" and lists the reasons why it is great.

If you say, I never get this right, it says "Yes", you never get this right and here are all the reasons why you don't....etc.

The subconscious mind always says "YES", agrees, accepts, then looks for evidence to support that assertion. Therefore, we must be careful what we say to ourselves.

Your subconscious mind loves you, so it always accepts anything you tell it. Then it rationalizes for you in order to be consistent and make you feel justified. If your subconscious mind argued with you every time you impressed a thought or impulse, you would be torn apart and could not function. You would likely jump off the first bridge you could find as your thought life would be intolerable.

Think about it. If every time you said, "I am a loser" and it would respond with "no you are not a loser, it is just that you are simply a lazy bum, the reason you lose is because you never try, and you don't care", etc. This would create an unsustainable condition. Therefore, your subconscious mind will not argue with you, it will agree, accept and rationalize on your behalf.

It is your conscious mind that has the ability to surface competing thoughts, beliefs, assessments, arguments, etc. And it is the conscious mind that must sort through these and determine which it will allow as the predominant programming that will be impressed on the subconscious mind.

The conscious mind has limited processing capability.
The subconscious mind has unlimited processing capability.

The subconscious mind is always ready and eager to automate any process (physical, mental, emotional) initiated by the conscious mind. The subconscious mind can perform any processes initiated by the conscious mind far better.

So now the question that begs to be asked is:

"What is the critical purpose and important functions of the conscious mind. What is that only it can do that the super powerhouse of the subconscious mind is unable to perform?

This is the million-dollar question. And the answer provides you with KEY insights and understanding of how you are to PROPERLY operate your conscious mind for the overall good and benefit of its user.... YOU!!!!

The following are the 3 MOST critical Empowerment roles and responsibilities of your conscious mind:

#1. The conscious mind must stand guard at the door. It must be the gate keeper of your thought life.

It must guard the subconscious mind from the outside world, it's influences, suggestions, beliefs, and impressions. Knowing that if those are "let in" to the subconscious mind they will take root and find a measure of realization and automation. Since the subconscious mind does not discern, judge, or question. It is TOTALLY open and accepting of everything it is offered. It simply says "Yes" and processes whatever is impressed upon it.

The conscious mind must guard to ensure the subconscious only receives positive, empowering, constructive input. This is extremely important. The conscious mind cannot allow the "keyboard" or "Input Ports" of this most powerful super computer, the subconscious mind, to be left unattended or used carelessly.

You would not leave the keyboard of your super computer out unattended for people to randomly come by and type in things like, "hate", "failure", "victim", etc..... You would also never hand over the controls of a rocket launcher or a powerful bazooka to a child. As these are too powerful and must only be used in a very responsible and purposeful way.

The conscious mind must stand guard at the door. It must be both the **discerner, and determiner** of what gets in. It determines the input that is allowed access and become impressed upon the super powerful subconscious mind. Our conscious mind should only allow positive and productive input that will be used by the subconscious mind for our EMPOWERMENT, well-being, and BENEFIT.

Not only is the conscious mind supposed to guard from outside influences, but it must also be on guard to ensure that the stream of our own conscious thoughts serve as POSITIVE and EMPOWERING input for our subconscious mind. For our ultimate benefit. To aid in our empowerment.

The conscious mind must decide and determine what thoughts and ideas are to be entertained and indulged. And what thoughts or ideas are to be rejected and ignored. The conscious mind must always be on guard. Always discerning and determining what thought programs will be allowed to run. And what paradigms and mindsets are accepted as true.

#2. The conscious mind must be the Captain. It must take charge.

Only the conscious mind can set the course or point the way. It must direct our focus, attention, intentions, and awareness. It is responsible for setting the INTENTIONS and PURPOSES that will be impressed upon the subconscious mind. It must be forceful, clear, and persistent in stating our truest wants and desires. It must continually impress upon our totally accepting and incredibly powerful subconscious mind our truest intentions and desires. It must do this consistently. Therefore, enabling the subconscious mind to process and act towards those intentions and desires in the powerful, amazing, and mysterious way that only the subconscious mind can.

#3. The conscious mind must IMAGINE, be CREATIVE, and VISUALIZE.

The conscious mind must use its imaginative and creative faculties in the process of determining and deciding our wants and desires. By using our creative and imaginative powers we impress upon the subconscious mind in a very powerful way. Our subconscious mind does NOT know the difference between something "real" and something imagined. Therefore, we must not be limited or constrained by our senses. As they can be very deceiving and limiting.

The conscious mind must control and direct the flow of our imaginings. Because to one degree or another we are always using our imagination. As it is our imagination that is continually "filling in the blanks" and tying together the continual flow of sensory input we receive, in order for us to create our conscious impressions and assessments of them. We don't really think about this, but to a great extent we are all actively using our imagination in all our daily activities. It is our imagination that provides the glue that holds together all the sense perceptions we process. Yes, our imagination is what fills in all the blanks as it pieces together all our external and internal sense perceptions into the final mental constructs that we ultimately assemble and accept as our reality.

The ability of the conscious mind to be creative and imaginative is incredibly important. Your imagination informs and inspires your "wants" which in turn ENERGIZE your "will". Thus, causing you to feel and act in ways that are consistent with your intentional desires and goals.

The conscious mind must be free and willing to utilize its full CREATIVITY and IMAGINATION in this endeavor of feeding the subconscious mind with powerful intentions of what you want to realize, achieve, and experience in your life.

The subconscious mind is in love with your conscious mind. It wants it to do what only it can do for the benefit of the one it serves. Because both your conscious and unconscious mind Love YOU !!!!They want you to be your EMPOWERED SELF!!!

Sadly, the following is a characterization of the conscious mind of most dis-empowered people: Their "front door" to the subconscious mind is like a half-broken screen door that is un latched and flapping in the wind. Letting in every silly, wrong, disempowering, unproductive message and impression from the outside world…from TV shows, movies, songs, etc. Allowing "in" all the complaints and negative mindset impressions from frustrated, hang-up ridden friends, relatives, neighbors, celebrities, politicians, teachers, you name it.

This "front door" is WIDE OPEN allowing whatever to get in and randomly push the buttons and set up disempowering programming on the super computer that is the subconscious mind. Talk about a perfect scenario for garbage in-garbage out. Does it surprise us that in this condition people can be prone to confusion, frustration, sadness, depression, un-fulfillment, and disempowerment?

Interestingly, the Hebrew word for "simple" or "fool" is derived from a root word that implies extreme vulnerability, literally meaning "to be opened up". This paints a picture of an "open door" with no means of active or reasonable discernment.

Additionally, for most people there is NO captain at the helm of their super computer. You ask most people what they want, and they can't tell you. If you press them they will, at best, offer up "fuzzy wishes" or wishful thinking. This is because they have NOT given serious, sustained, directed thought to determining their wants, purposes and desires.

Many of us are confused, aimless and purposeless. Simply going through the motions in life. Barely just "showing up" or showing up "wrong". Like going to the Academy Awards presentation dressed in a swim suit. Aim-less, purpose-less, pointless.... POWER LESS!!!!!

Without a captain to give it direction, a jet plane or giant cruise ship simply flounders and goes nowhere. Rather than travel in the wonderful way for which they were designed. We are designed to live EMPOWERED lives filled with purpose, achievement, fulfillment, and continual growth. We are POWER-FULL, not POWER-LESS.

There is a motivational quote that says: "It is not that most people aim high and miss, it is that they aim low and hit". It is more accurate to state it this way: "It is not that most people aim high and miss, or even that they aim low and hit. BUT that they are NOT aiming AT ALL. And then, they complain and fuss about not hitting anything at all."

We have these powerful tools at our disposal and we are carelessly and haplessly wielding them. We have not become masterful in the art of utilizing and directing our conscious and subconscious mind.

This condition that most disempowered people exhibit reminds me of a section from Alice in Wonderland where Alice is speaking to Cat.

Cat: Where are you going?

Alice: Which way should I go?

Cat: That depends on where you are going.

Alice: I don't know

Cat: Then it does not matter which way you go

Lewis Carroll, Alice in Wonderland (Alice's Adventures in Wonderland, #1)

For your ONE mind to function towards your full benefit and empowerment the conscious mind MUST effectively play its role. The subconscious mind is always awake and faithfully working to its full capacity. However, it is the conscious mind that tends to be lazy and unguarded. We must become more disciplined in our conscious thinking. This is necessary work that we must do in order to unleash our Empowered Self.

"You are today where your thoughts have brought you; you will be tomorrow where your thoughts take you."

James Allen

What Is Real?

In this section, we will be covering an important area of your belief system that you may never have consciously considered. This is a topic that may at first seem a bit esoteric and impractical, but it is just the opposite. Once understood and embraced it will prove to be very obvious, practical, and impactful. Extremely important in properly shaping your Empowered mindset and understanding.

As I have noted several times before, a key objective of the empowerment journey is to embrace more truth. And as we understand and embrace more truth, whether about the world around us or ourselves, we grow in our empowerment. Because truth is powerful. As truth leads to right understanding and greater wisdom that then leads to right thinking and right action.

In this section, the aim is to shed a new and greater light in an area of our understanding that is foundational to developing a more empowered mindset. When more light is shed on something there is more "seeing". In that greater light, you are able to see things more clearly and in greater detail.

The following discussion will cause you to think differently and, in the process, enable you to develop a more empowered mindset and world view. I guarantee that you will have some serious "Ah-ha" moments in this section that follows.

Let's begin this enlightening exercise by asking a simple but profound question: What is real? The typical response to this question usually sounds something like this: "If it is physical and visible it is REAL if it is NOT physical and visible, it is NOT real". Most people would promptly agree with this definition. Wouldn't you?

Let us now reason together to see if this definition holds up under further consideration. Consider the following: Is gravity real? Is heat real? Are radio waves real? Is electricity real? We know the answer to be "YES". Of course, these things are real. They have very real, practical, and objective effects in our lives. These are all real things that we know exist, but we cannot see. However, even though we can't see them, they affect our daily lives in very significant ways. So, we must accept them as "Real". They are invisible, non-physical things. But they are quite real.

Let's go a bit further and ask, "Is love real? Is hate real?" Yes, and Yes…We also accept these as real. Since they also have very real effects on our lives. While these may be less objective than the things previously mentioned, they nonetheless affect us in deep ways. Again, they are invisible and non-physical, but they are quite real.

So, when you stop and think about it, you understand that love, hate, joy, etc. are invisible and non-physical things, but they are real. Just like heat, gravity, electricity, etc. Since we accept these things as real, we can no longer hold on to the false belief that says: "What is physical and visible is real, and what is not physical or visible is not real". We must now promptly correct this definition to say: "Real things can be both visible, and invisible, physical and non-physical. Many of the things we know to be REAL are NOT physical or visible…but they are still REAL".

Keep in mind that in this section I am not attempting to completely and objectively define all the things that can be cataloged as “REAL” in any broad, practical, or philosophical sense. As this would likely deserve an entire book. However, for the purpose of our empowerment conversation, I do aim to expose some wrong and disempowering thinking in our belief system regarding what we consider to be real and not real. And how this wrong thinking greatly impacts our world and self-view in limiting ways.

Now you know and can accept that there are many invisible things that are REAL. Because these invisible things have very real and significant effects on the subjective, and objective experiences in our lives.

So, let’s keep going a bit further and talk about actual “things” versus the concept or idea of “things”. Let me ask you, “What is more real, the chair you sit on in the morning while having breakfast or the idea, the concept of “chair”?

Most of us would answer consistent with our old limiting and wrong paradigm that says the chair we sit on is more real than the idea or concept of chair. Well. let’s also challenge and expose this limiting, narrow, and wrong understanding.

Think about it. In a few hundred years, will the chair you now sit on still be “real”? The answer is no, because we know that in a few hundred years that chair would have likely long disappeared. The materials that make up that chair would have deteriorated and disintegrated. As result of the natural physical effects of rusting, rotting, etc.

These processes are not really a disintegration but more accurately, a transformation. Because at the molecular level, the materials that make up the physical chair naturally transition to become a part of something else. Those molecules will, through natural, physical processes, or by the actions of man transform and transition into other things; dirt, air, flowers, a new chair, other things altogether, etc.....

All visible things will eventually “disappear”. As they will cease to be that particular “thing”. And their component parts inevitably become part of other “things”. As all physical things are made up from the same “soup” of molecules, atoms, electrons, etc. that continually flow to form all the “stuff” in our visible universe. Continually transitioning from stuff to other stuff. Through the normal processes of nature or through processes initiated by man.

We know that there is a conservation of energy and matter. As matter is neither created or destroyed. It is merely always changing form.

So, we agree that in a few hundred years that chair will most likely no longer exist as a chair. But, let me ask you, what about the idea or concept of a chair. Will this concept still be real? Of course, the concept will be real as long as there is a conscious, thinking mind that can conceive the idea of a chair. And, as long as the concept can be conceived, a new chair can always be produced or REAL…ized. Made “real”.

So, what is more real? The physical chair that we can see for a brief span of time, or the idea, the concept of chair, which is timeless? The physical, visible things have a definite lifespan. But the invisible concepts from where the physical things are born are timeless.

“What is real is not the external form, but the essence of things”
Constantin Brancusi

Accepting this powerful and inescapable truth gives us a strong foundation that allows us to think about and understand the world around us more deeply, more correctly, and with a more empowered mindset. You see, when we use the words “real” versus “not real” this creates a limiting and wrong paradigm. The correct way to understand these concepts is to think about things as **realized, and not realized**.

This is a very important distinction in how we should think and speak about things. As this is a more enlightened and correct way of thinking. Because if there is a mind that can conceive of a thing. That thing can become REAL-ized. But there must first be the mind that can conceive and imagine the invisible idea for the idea to have the power to become visible and physical.

With this new, enlightened thinking now take a look all around you. Do you realize that you are literally surrounded by materialized thoughts and ideas? Yes, ALL that you see, that man has made, was first an idea or a thought. All the visible things that you see all around you had their beginning, their birth, in the invisible form as a thought, or idea. Absolutely everything that man has made, without exception, had its origin as an invisible idea that was then made real…or Real-ized

Everything in your house. The walls, carpets, microwave, tv, phone, etc.…started out as an idea. Then became realized through a corresponding process. You are even wearing materialized ideas that have been purposely realized as clothes. This book is an idea that has been very purposely realized. When you drive your car, you are driving many ideas that were put together, and materialized for your driving pleasure. Do you "see" this now?

This applies to everything in the man-made world. Again, look all around you and understand that everything you see is **materialized mind stuff**. We are surrounded by the realized and materialized ideas of other people. Everything we see and experience as "real" in the man-made world, are thoughts and ideas that have been intentionally and purposely realized and materialized.

Everything that has been realized had to first start as an invisible thought or idea. And only then was it possible for it to become realized in a visible and physical way.

Is this realization shocking to you? Yes, it is shocking because this is not how you have been taught to view the world. But it is true, and it is obvious. Now that you think about it, you agree and accept it. This leads us to understand something that is EXTREMELY obvious and fundamental, but that you have possibly never considered quite this way.

The visible comes from the invisible

This visible world that we are so familiar with, and that we assume is our ultimate reality, is fundamentally a product of the ideas and thoughts that are first formed in the creative and imaginative mind.

The visible world flows inevitably, necessarily, and continually from the invisible world. How is that for a mindset and paradigm change? Yes, we must transition from a materially minded paradigm to a more immaterially minded paradigm. From physical mindset, to a spiritual mindset.

"So, we fix our eyes not on what is seen, but in what is unseen, since what is seen is temporary, but what is unseen is eternal"
2 Cor 4:18

Initially you believed that things were only real if you could see and touch them. Now you know and understand that to see and touch it, you must FIRST conceive the thought or idea. You now have a more correct and empowered mindset.

This reminds us of the saying "I'll believe it when I see it". But now you understand how flawed this is. Because now it is obvious that if you never conceive it or believe it…you will never see it. Since the visible flows from and is born from the invisible. We must first believe it before we will ever see it. The only reason you can see it is because someone first conceived it, believed it, and then real..ized it.

So, the logical implication of this is that …. just like gravity, heat, or love. Thoughts and ideas are "REAL". It can be rightly stated that thoughts and ideas are actual "Things".

Thoughts and ideas are real, they are things!!!

Thoughts and ideas are the precursors to all that we see and experience. This is not spooky, mystical, or strange. This is just the way it is. And now that you think about it, you understand it is true, and obvious. Let me repeat…not only is it true…but it is OBVIOUS. Thoughts and ideas are the necessary precursors to all that we see AND experience. Do you see it more clearly now?

It may help to think of it this way. Thoughts are seeds. We just agreed that everything we see started out as a thought first. It didn't just come out of nowhere for no reason. It originated from a specific thought or idea. So, our thoughts and ideas are seeds that contain the potential to realize the specific thing that is thought of or imagined.

ALL that you see around you, that man has made, started out in seed form as a thought. And then became realized by means of a specific process and favorable conditions. Every thought has the potential to become the thing imagined or believed. Thoughts are the seeds of the stuff we see in the outer, physical world.

**Just like every seed has the potential
to become the specific tree or plant
Every thought carries with it the potential
to realize the thing imagined or believed.**

This is FUNDAMENTAL!!! This understanding must form a key part of the foundation of your empowerment thinking. Because this understanding has radical implications in your daily living.

You now understand why the conscious mind MUST stand guard at the door of your thinking. Because every thought or idea is truly like a seed being planted in the garden of your life. That has the potential to become REALIZED. The only things that have the potential to become realized are the things that are first seeded in thought. It is the thought, the idea of the thing, that contains within it the very potential to realize that specific thing.

If you are growing apples it is because you have planted apple seeds…if you are growing plums, it is because plum seeds were planted. If you see a chair it is because someone first imagined and thought of a chair. They planted the idea of a chair, and through a certain process that "seed" of a chair idea was realized to become the physical chair.

But wait, let's keep going…. If you are experiencing frustration it must also follow that it is because you planted "frustration seeds". If you are experiencing failure at work it is because you have been planting "failure seeds". If your relationships are filled with arguments and anger…. you now know the reason… it is because you have been planting seeds of argument and anger.

This simple understanding can and MUST be applied to everything in our lives. This is a UNIVERSAL PRINCIPLE. The principle of cause, process, and effect. Of reaping and sowing.

Thoughts and ideas are the seeds containing the potentiality for all of the physical and visible objective outcomes and realities

So, watch out!!!! Pay attention!!! Stand Guard…Think about what you think about!!!!

As we discussed in a prior chapter, everything happens for a reason. This is obvious. It is a settled fact established by the law of cause and effect. Every effect has a cause. Every cause has an effect. You simply cannot have one without the other. They are inevitably, intrinsically, and inescapably linked. Thoughts and ideas are the primary cause…the things they produce are the effects.

Get this, the "outside" world…this visible, physical world that we think we know so well is merely the AFTER EFFECT of the invisible world…ALL the stuff we see, AND experience is the after effect of the invisible stuff we think about!!! Individually and collectively.

"The power of thought, of idea,
is incommensurable, is immeasurable.
The world is dominated by thought"
Emile Coue

The VISIBLE comes from the INVISIBLE. For anything to have the power to become physical and visible it must first exist in an invisible state of potential. Just like a tree will NOT grow unless a seed was planted, nothing can be realized unless a thought was first "planted".

You are planting the seeds in YOUR life. And YOU are working the process, creating, and allowing the conditions in YOUR life that are producing the effects in YOUR life

We spend most if not all our time focused on, responding to, and worrying about the effects in our lives. Never truly realizing that we are planting the seeds that are the CAUSE of all the effects in our lives. We are too reliant on the senses which only have the power to perceive that which has already been caused. Instead we should be more focused on the invisible states of intention and potential. As this is the cradle for all our future objective creations. This is where we have the power to create. By sowing a new reality, therefore a new potential future chain of events of our own intentional purposes.

Our intentions and purposeful choosing is where we create. They will become the causation for the things we will experience and realize in the future. Empowerment Rule #7: Your Intentionality Determines Your Potentiality.

We have sadly become predominantly programmed to be more focused on the effects in our lives rather than on the causes. The causes are the mindsets, intentions, thoughts, and ideas that we persistently hold. We live bound to and obsessed by the after effects.

We perpetuate this disempowering and victimizing cycle of responding to the effect, of the effect, of the effect…We become a negative echo that keeps on repeating. With no hope of escaping this relentless and endless disempowering loop.

We must wake up and realize that we ARE the effective cause. That we are the ones planting or allowing others to plant the seeds that will grow to produce the experiences and outcomes in our lives.

We do not always plant consciously. As much of our planting happens subconsciously from old patterns of thought that no longer serve us in positive or productive ways. Furthermore, often the seeds are being planted by outside influences or people. Without our direct or even conscious consent.

Now you see why we must SHOUT OUT to our conscious mind… “GUARD THE DOOR!!!” We must NOT allow ANY unwanted seed to be planted in the fertile garden of our mind and emotions. Because once they become impressed in our subconscious, they will inevitably lead us toward experiencing the effects of those very impressions. They have the power to become the objective realities that we will we realize and experience to lesser or greater degrees in our lives.

At the same time, we must direct our conscious mind to "GRAB HOLD OF THE WHEEL". Be the CAPTAIN. Be present and intentional in all things. It is the job and the DUTY of our conscious mind to be in charge of establishing clear intentions in every area of our lives. To CHOOSE with INTENTIONALITY the things we want. To respond in every situation in an empowered way. To censor the outside influences and to allow only positive enabling, intentional "cause" seeds to be planted in our life.

We must be guarded in our thinking and purposeful in our intentions. That is the highest responsibility of our conscious mind.

Think about what you think about. Do not let others think for you, or influence your thinking in negative, disempowering ways. Guard your thinking, guard your emotions. Direct your intentions and continually inform your mindset with the purposeful wants and desires that will benefit you. Become Master of yourself.

"One can have no greater mastery than mastery of oneself"
Leonardo daVinci

Your life is like your garden…You must be a mindful gardener. Only plant positive, encouraging, empowering seeds in the garden of your mind. Consciously choose what seeds you will plant where and when. Once planted they must be noticed, nourished, and cared for over time so they can become strong and REALized in your life.

Your thoughts, beliefs, ideas, desires, are seeds you continually plant in your mind. And these will eventually sprout, grow, and become the substance of your life.

If you do not like the fruit, vegetables, or weeds that you are growing in your garden, then STOP that sowing.... Decide what fruits and vegetables you want to enjoy and go “find” those “seeds”. Start thinking different thoughts, desiring different things, imagining, and feeling different things. Seeding the different realities that you desire.

Guard your garden. Be selective about the thoughts and attitudes you hold. Be selective about the outside influences that you allow to sow seeds in your garden. Be more aware how the following influence your thinking and attitudes: friends, family, neighbors, TV shows, music, etc....

It is that simple. However, understandably, it may take time for you to master these simple truths. But be encouraged and know that it is only you that is in charge of YOU. And you can take more charge, more control, as you become more mindful and more intentional in every area of your life.

Convince yourself of these truths and embrace them as your new thinking and believing. This new and correct thinking will help you to understand and accept the following Empowerment rules. So, let me now introduce you to the next set of Empowerment rules......Enjoy!!!

Empowerment Rule #6

What You Focus On You Will Find

"Always remember, your focus determines your reality"
George Lucas

Anything that you consistently think about, you will, to some degree, inevitably realize and experience in your life. What you focus on you will find…

We all have our own personal way of seeing ourselves and the world around us. Our very own unique and individual worldview. And it is this unique self and world-view that shapes and determines who we are, and who we are becoming.

It is how and what we think that ultimately differentiates us from one another. We are basically and fundamentally a product of our thinking. Because it is our thinking that ultimately and inevitably produces the outward realities that we experience.

"We become what we think about most of the time"
Earl Nightingale

It is our thinking that shapes and directs how we feel, respond, speak, and act. Our bodies are an instrument for our mind. Our biological make-up is only the conduit for our thought life. It is therefore our thinking that ultimately defines who we are and how we live. And ultimately determines what we realize and experience in every area of our lives.

***"The body is the servant of the mind.
It obeys the operations of the mind,
whether they be deliberately chosen
or automatically expressed"***
James Allen

The conscious and subconscious thoughts, ideas, and beliefs that you persistently hold in your mind will produce the feelings, emotions, words, and actions that you will eventually realize and experience. Your thought life becomes manifested in your outer life, as the visible inevitably flows from the invisible.

Whatever you believe and think about continually, you will draw into and out of your life. This is what makes your life different than mine. You think different, believe different, desire different and therefore realize and experience a different life than mine or anyone else.

***"A man is literally what he thinks,
his character being the complete sum
of all his thoughts"***
James Allen

Our thoughts are the effective cause of all the subjective and objective effects we experience. What we continually plant in the soil of our mind will become real in the garden of our lives. Because every thought, like a seed, has the potential to realize the very thing it conceives.

Just as the apple seed carries within it the potential to realize an apple tree. It is the same with EACH thought we think. They are seeds containing the potential to realize the very substance of that particular thought.

We know that an apple tree must always be preceded by an apple seed, and so it is that all our objective realities must always be preceded by the invisible "seed" energies that bring them forth. Every objective effect that becomes realized must be preceded by the invisible thought energy that contains the seed potential to realize that objective effect.

Without the seed there is no tree. Without the thought or idea there is no physical representation of that thought or idea. Remember that thoughts are real things. They are the precursors to the visible. Therefore, what you think and believe is what you will inevitably realize, experience, and become. As your thoughts and emotions are the virtual seeds that you continually plant and that take root to bear their corresponding fruit in your life.

"What you focus on grows,
what you think about expands,
and what you dwell upon
determines your destiny"
Robin Sharma

This principle of "What we focus on we find" is also true because of our natural inclination to be drawn to the things we persistently think about. You are naturally more likely to notice, encounter, and experience those things that you have cultivated and entertained in your thinking. The thoughts you persist in will develop in you a stronger bias and preference for those very things.

For example; If you often think about chocolate ice cream, you will most likely be tempted to buy some next time you are at the grocery store. And, consequently, you will likely eat some during the week. Conversely, if you do not think about chocolate ice cream, you will likely NOT buy some and will likely NOT eat any this week.

This is a very simple example of the reality that what you focus on you find. What you focus on you will likely experience because you have expressed a preference for it, and you are therefore more inclined to take steps towards experiencing it.

We are "drawn" to the things we hold in our thoughts. As the thought images are the virtual seeds that must eventually find expression in a physical form. This is a normal progression that to one degree or another, applies to everything in life. Yes, what you focus on you will find.

Subconscious Filtering

We are all more receptive, and welcoming to, the thoughts and ideas we have accepted and persistently hold in our minds. For instance, if you have an interest in fashion and health, as you look through a magazine stand you will be drawn to the fashion and health magazines. Those magazines will literally "jump out" at you from the magazine stand. Conversely, if you have no interest in the subject of fishing, as you look through that same magazine stand, you will likely not even "see" any of the fishing magazines. They will be "invisible" to you as your subconscious mind will choose to filter them out of your conscious view. Because your subconscious knows that they are not important to you.

Whatever it is that you have determined a preference for you will tend to filter IN to your awareness and experience. Conversely, the things you do not prefer you will tend to filter OUT. This is one of the key functions of your subconscious mind. It acts as a filter. It will actively filter IN to your conscious "view" the things it believes are important to you. And, it will filter OUT of your conscious "view" the things it believes are not important to you. Filtering is a normal and necessary function of our subconscious mind.

The reason why subconscious "filtering" is practical and necessary is because there is always an overwhelming, ever present amount of "free data" available for us to perceive, assess, and process.

As the world around us continually offers millions of bits of available information that we can process at any given time. And being that our conscious mind can only process a limited amount of information at one time, the subconscious mind (which has the ability to process a far greater amount of information at one time) must serve as the FILTER for the conscious mind.

It does this as a necessary function to protect us from becoming overwhelmed. To prevent us from sensory overload. So, what does the subconscious mind do? It filters in consistent with what it believes is most necessary for us in every circumstance. What it believes is important to us. It does this because it is our mind, and it wants to please us. It wants the best for us. It is only doing what it believes we want or desire. It will not filter in the things it does not believe are of interest or importance to us. So, those things that we do not focus on, or think about, we will likely not find.

One simple and common example of how the subconscious mind filters for us is evident in what happens when you buy a new car. Once you buy a specific car you now tend to notice them literally everywhere. Prior to your purchase you may not have noticed them. But now, suddenly, they are everywhere you look. What is happening is not that, all the sudden, there are more of them on the road. But that your subconscious mind is now filtering them in to your conscious awareness. Because you have impressed upon your subconscious mind that this car is important to you. Therefore, you will notice them more and more. Whatever you focus on you will find.

Over time you have impressed upon your subconscious mind the things that are important to you. How have you done this? By your predominant thoughts, and emotions. By the things you continually and persistently allow yourself to think about. By the beliefs and paradigms that you hold and have accepted as true about yourself and about the world around you.

Whether they are positive or negative, empowering or disempowering, true or false. Whatever things you have accepted as true, and real, must, to some degree, find their objectified, empirical equivalent in your life. This is a natural law.

Seek and Ye Shall Find

What is the logical conclusion of seeking? The logical, unavoidable conclusion to seeking, is finding. If you do not stop looking for something you will eventually find it. This is fundamental. If it exists, it can be found. And it is true that all things exist, either in a physical reality or in a state of potential reality (more to come on this).

If you have a deep belief that positive outcomes will happen. Your subconscious will filter in information that supports that belief and will inevitably "find" the positive outcomes. However, if you continually believe and expect that negative or "bad" things will happen, the subconscious mind will also inevitably "find" and allow those things to filter in so that you can realize what it is that you expect and "desire".

"What you think about, you bring about"
Les Brown

If you believe that the world is an unfair place, you will find more and more evidence to support this belief. Since this is your bias. If you believe that people are "out to get you" you will also find that this is true. As your subconscious mind will be "looking" for more evidence of this in your life to support your belief.

If you believe that you will never achieve success, then your subconscious mind will find and rationalize for you all the reasons why you cannot or will not succeed.

Likewise, if you believe that all things will eventually "work out" for the best, then that becomes the pattern you will find and bring to reality as you experience events in your life. You will find that all things do eventually work themselves out for the best. What you focus on you will find.

Remember, your subconscious mind only wants to please you. It is nonjudgmental. It will accept whatever it is that you propose to it by way of your continual, conscious thoughts, ideas, beliefs, and mental attitudes.

Once the subconscious mind has been impressed upon, it begins to work in very efficient and mysterious ways to seek out and thus, realize those very things that have been impressed upon it. Your thoughts and beliefs establish the framework for what you will inevitably realize and experience.

So, you see, this process is important to understand and direct in more conscious empowering ways. Because this mechanism will work either way. So here again we are reminded of the power of choosing and thus the ability for us to determine a more empowered way forward on the path of life.

As you consciously and persistently fill your mind with positive, empowered thoughts, paradigms, and beliefs, these will become more embedded into your subconscious. And over time these will become the default programming that will run in you conscious and subconscious mind. And you will in turn become more inclined to realize and experience the objective realties that are consistent with those beliefs.

Knowing this to be true you must take charge of your thinking and become more conscious and intentional. You must be mindful of any negative or disempowering mindsets. Think about what you think about. Challenge and change any limiting or disempowering thought pattern or belief system that you may have allowed yourself to create or have embraced over time.

Your limiting beliefs will limit you,
and your empowering beliefs will empower you.

Most of our challenges in becoming more empowered lie in our ability to undo the negative thought and parading patterns that we have formed over time. We all have many disempowering and limiting beliefs that have been etched in our pattern of thinking and feeling over the course of our lives.

These negative and disempowering beliefs are buried deep in our subconscious mind and have silently become part of our operating system. Most of us need a complete new operating system download. A software update with the latest features and programs that can enable our hardware to run more effectively and in a more empowered way.

This is what the content of this book aims to provide. New updated software programming that will enable you to run more efficient and empowering belief programs that will result in more positive, productive, thoughts, feelings, emotions, and actions. That will, in turn, result in more positive and powerful outcomes.

To a great degree our lives are a self-fulfilling prophecy. Because whatever it is that you believe, and desire will create in you a very real and strong bias for finding and experiencing those very things. And these are the things your conscious and subconscious mind will accept, identify, and construct from the millions of bits of information that are always available to us in any situation or circumstance in our lives.

The stuff that exists in your life you have attracted and welcomed. Your mind is the welcome mat of your life. It says "I have been thinking about you, and now here you are. Come into my life, you are welcomed". The problem with this is that the thing "welcomed" may not be something you truly want or desire. It may be a "good" or a "bad" thing. But it is welcomed nonetheless because you have brought it about by way of your persistent thoughts or intentions.

It is empowering for you to understand, accept, and embrace that what you are is simply the outward projection of your internal thought choices and beliefs. What you cultivate on the inside will become the harvest that will be produced on the outside. And you have the power to change at any time that you purposely, intentionally, and persistently decide to do so.

Here, once again, you must be reminded that all your thoughts and beliefs are choices that you make. And, you can choose to change your thoughts, beliefs, and desires any time you determine to. Remember Empowerment Rule #5: You Have the Power to Choose.

"You must first change your mind, before you can change your life."

When you make purposeful, intentional choices you are turning the key that enables and reveals your true self. Your Empowered Self. Your choices ultimately reveal who you are, and who you are becoming.

If you have always believed yourself to be unfriendly, someone who does not easily make friends. You can consciously choose to become friendlier, and more approachable. Once that clear choice is intentionally made, and held persistently in the conscious mind, you will impress this unto your subconscious.

Then, over time, you will inevitably start to realize this new you. Assuming you purposely stay in that intentional choice. If you do, then this new mind attitude will start to change who you identify yourself to be. It will energize new emotions and feelings which will start to cause a change in your actions, which in turn changes your experiences and outcomes.

Once your deep-seated beliefs change, the outward changes are inevitable. It is just a matter of time, because the outer will ALWAYS reflect the inner. As the visible flows from the invisible.

If you have always accepted and believed yourself to be overweight and unhealthy, you can right now choose to change. But you must first do this through your ability to change your mindset. Mindset management must come first, before the physical reality will follow.

You will limit, deny, and prevent yourself for as long as you accept and persist in your current disempowered mindset. Since you will only ever produce and realize consistent with your current mindset.

Therefore, mindset management is key. Because when we change what is inside us, the outer will inevitably, over time, reflect this change. It must, as the visible always flows from the invisible. The outer reflects the inner.

Everything we “seek” already exists, either in a physical reality or in a state of potentiality. This is the reason why we will always find that which we earnestly and persistently seek. Because it already exists in some form.

This is just as fundamental as the truth of reaping and sowing. If you want to enjoy a specific fruit you must plant that specific seed. When you plant a seed, you will eventually enjoy the fruit that it produces. When we seek, we are planting thought seeds that we will eventually find as materialized or emotional realities.

Our lives are a creation of our own making. However, one of the reasons why we may fail to see this more clearly is because our thoughts, like seeds, do not fully mature and grow instantly. For seeds to yield their fruit they must go through an appropriate process and be in a favorable condition. This process involves time. The element of time cannot be avoided or ignored as every cause and effect must work itself out by way of the process of time.

Therefore, as we experience the effects in our lives which have been unavoidably brought about by our own thoughts (mindset). And since our thoughts and the corresponding results they inevitably produce are separated by time, we fail to clearly see their interconnection. We thus mistakenly explain away the effects in our lives as the result of chance or mere circumstance. Rather that understanding the truth of the matter, that we are simply experiencing the very fruits of our own making.

"Man is buffeted by circumstances
so long as he believes himself
to be the creature of outside conditions,
but when he realizes that he is a creative power,
and that he commands the hidden soil and
seeds of his being out of which circumstances grow,
he then becomes the rightful master of himself"
James Allen

Your thoughts are the starting point for all you will experience and realize in your life. Because your thought life establishes the invisible framework that will become realized over time. For something to become manifested as physical and visible, there must first exist the mental or invisible framework for it. All physical creation can only come about after a mental image has first been formed. A building needs a blueprint before it can be constructed. All physical images must first have a spiritual image. The Invisible precedes the visible

The Empowered person must be master of their thoughts. To the degree that you master and control your thoughts is to the degree that you will master your life. You must become mindful, in order to be masterful.

"The mind is a beautiful servant,
but a dangerous master"
Osho

Always remember that a KEY function of your conscious mind is to stand guard at the door. This means you must be ready and alert to actively monitor, censor, and direct your thoughts and stream of consciousness to align with your true desires, beliefs, and intentions.

Practice the art of thinking about what you think about. Being mindful to become masterful. Directing your stream of thought intentionally and purposely. DO not allow yourself to be swept away by negative, disempowering, purposeless thinking. Your thoughts determine your emotions which will inspire your actions which will produce your results.

So, let us recap…….

What you focus on you will find, because…

#1. Your thoughts are seeds being planted in the garden of your life. They will eventually take root and inevitably bear their corresponding fruit. Your invisible thoughts must and will produce after their own kind.

#2. You are naturally drawn to the things you think about or have an interest in. Your mind acts like a like honing device. Continually drawing you and bringing you towards the thoughts, and beliefs that you prefer and persistently hold in your conscious and subconscious attention.

#3. You are impressing your subconscious mind by your persistent and predominant thoughts, beliefs, desires, etc. So, the amazing subconscious mind will continually "look" for the things you have impressed upon it. As part of the process it will filter in or out of your conscious "field of view" those things it believes are important or not important to you. It will therefore cause you to find more of the very things it believes you want or prefer. Whether you have impressed upon it in an intentional or unintentional way.

Empowerment Habit:

Be Positive

"You Can't live a positive life with a negative mind"

I AM... POSITIVE. I always choose to find, embrace, and maintain the most positive, empowered perspective in any and every situation. This is my default programming.

Empowerment starts with the choice to BE POSITIVE. To think positive, to live positive. This is a foundational empowerment habit. Because you simply cannot experience a positive life if you are indulging in negative thinking. Period. End of story. Therefore, being positive must become one of the strongest habits and foremost characteristic of the empowered individual.

To be empowered you must cultivate a positive mindset and make the continual conscious decision to not indulge in negative or defeated thinking. You must program yourself to become a positive thought machine. Simply refuse to indulge in negative thoughts, ideas, conversations, etc. Because they will rob you of your power and surely drag you in a downward, disempowered direction.

What you focus on you will find, and eventually realize in your life. Thoughts are real, and they will reproduce after their own kind. Negative thoughts will only produce negative emotions which will result in negative outcomes.

When the subconscious mind offers up a negative thought, it's ok. Remember that simply having a negative thought or being in a negative mindset is not the problem. The problems are created when we allow ourselves to consciously and consistently entertain those negative thoughts.

The problems develop when we breathe life into our negativity by persisting in those thoughts and allowing them to take root. Yes, your subconscious mind may be sending them out there, but it is your CONSCIOUS mind that can decide what to do next. And here is where you must make the conscious decision to NOT indulge or entertain them. Do not allow them the power of your attention.

"Where attention goes, energy flows"
Anthony Robins

Remember that thoughts are real. They carry with them the potential to realize the very object of the thought. So, do NOT plant negative seed in the garden of your life. If you DO NOT plant the negative seeds, there will NOT be any negative fruit. It's really that simple. And if you do happen to plant a negative seed, remember that it still needs a favorable condition and process for it to grow. Starve your negative thoughts and inclinations. Deprive them of water and sunshine...They will wither and die.

<u>The Two Wolves</u>

An old Cherokee told his grandson:
"My son there is a battle between two wolves inside us all.
One is Evil. It is anger, jealousy, greed, resentment,
inferiority, lies and ego.
The other is Good. It is joy, peace, love, hope, humility,
kindness, empathy, and truth."
The boy thought about it and asked,
"Grandfather, which wolf wins?"
The old man quietly replied,
"The one you feed."

Author unknown

Will you at times have negative thoughts? Of course, you will. You can expect that your subconscious mind will continue to routinely offer them up. They will still crop up when you least expect or desire them. The reasons for this are buried deep in your subconscious programming. Remember that you may have allowed negative thought patterns to develop over many, many years of unintentional, purposeless, powerless thinking.

You cannot undo in one instant the habits and programming that have built up over a lifetime. It will not happen overnight, but it will get better over time. You will have victory in the end. You will become more positive if it is your intention to be so.

Engage your higher self and assert your intentionality that you do NOT want to embrace those negative thoughts. Let them go, send them packing. Consistently remind yourself that NOTHING POSITIVE comes out of SOMETHING NEGATIVE.

Having negative thoughts is very much like being on fire. If you do not take immediate action you will be consumed by the flames. So, treat the negative thoughts the same way you would treat being on fire. To prevent from becoming seriously burned you must…

STOP, DROP, & ROLL:

STOP the negative thoughts from taking over your mindset, attitude, or emotions.

DROP them from your consideration.

ROLL into a more positive thought, attitude, mindset, or emotion.

Know that your subconscious is only offering up those negative thoughts or emotions because you have allowed it to become programmed to do so. It is only doing what it believes you want. Since in the past, you have entertained those negative feelings, ideas, thoughts, or emotions it should not surprise you that they are still being offered up by your subconscious mind.

Your subconscious mind is not trying to undermine you. It only wants the best for you. It is your mind and it loves you. Accept it or not, it is only doing what it believes you want. If you are having negative thoughts it must be because you have allowed and indulged them in the past. They have become the path of least resistance for you because of the patterns you have allowed to become impressed upon your subconscious mind over the years.

Remember that the power of precedent is very real. This means that anytime you react a certain way; whether in thought, action, or emotion. This now sets a precedent and the subconscious mind, believing this is the preferred response, will tend to groove that into its programming. And it now becomes an automatic response, the path of least resistance, that no longer needs the approval of your conscious mind to initiate it. It simply runs as an automated response. But, you can begin to separate yourself from that pattern and start to form new ones.

The first step has already begun, you are self-aware and more intentional. You can decide to change the flow of your subconscious stream of thought. Take control because you are in control. Your conscious mind is the captain. Be strong minded and insist on the mindsets that you want to embrace. Focus not on what you have been, but on what, and who you are becoming.

“The secret of change is to focus all of your energy, not on fighting the old, but on building the new”
Socrates

If you are having the same persistent negative thoughts or emotions over and over, it is because the subconscious mind believes this is how you want to feel. It believes that these are the thoughts and mindset that you are familiar and comfortable with. So, it just plays that same program, the same routines for you.

This presents an opportunity for introspection. For you to honestly assess and understand why these thoughts are still part of your mindset. Why are you are still hanging on and allowing them to bend you this way and that way?

What is it about your character or inclinations that these negative thoughts are pointing to? There may be an element of you that needs to change. Think about that and you will gain new insight about any deeply held belief that you must let go of and change. Maybe it is a specific personality flaw that you now must take ownership for and determine to overcome.

The power of your intentionality is what will start the process and eventually gain for you a new victory. Your intentionality determines your potentiality (Rule #7). You can change if you determine to. Again, it will not happen overnight, but it will happen over time. Allow yourself the room and the time for it to happen…it WILL.

One typical negative train of thought that many people tend to have is the temptation and tendency to expect and anticipate that bad things will happen. That things will inevitably go wrong for us. Sadly, we often take on the Murphy's Law way of thinking that says, "Anything that can go wrong will go wrong".

Maybe this has to do with our need to survive that we tend to have negative thoughts anticipating negative or disastrous outcomes. But I say shift your purpose from survive, to THRIVE. Survival will take care of itself.

"Worrying is using your imagination
to create something you do not want."
Esther Hicks

You must NOT allow this to be your default thinking. You must anticipate and expect positive things. You must, by means of your own imagination, plant in your mind the positive outcomes you desire in any and every situation. Make this an intentional habit. Say to yourself: "I will continually program myself to expect and anticipate the best possible outcomes in any and every situation. I deserve this. I will not allow myself to be taken down the path of anxiety and dread. I will be a hopeful anticipator. This is my intention, my choosing."

Breaking Negative Thought or Emotional Patterns

Many times, the reason why we experience negative thoughts or emotions is because, in some way, we still want to indulge in them. We take some strange solace in our "victim" mentality. We want to be pitied. We choose to believe we have been wronged. So, we indulge those negative patterns. Here you must make a choice. Be honest with yourself. Why are you angry, depressed, etc.? Do you want to be? Have this mental conversation with yourself. You must start the process of undoing this negative pattern that you wish to re-direct.

What are you continually saying to yourself, what is your self-talk? What thought loops and thinking patterns are you programmed to run? Are you monitoring your self-talk and directing it in positive empowering ways? The rules and habits covered in this book will serve to help change your internal conversations, paradigms, and beliefs in more empowering ways.

Use positive affirmations. Say them out loud if you desire. Be your own self's biggest positive influence. There is a very real power in positive auto suggestion and positive self-talk.

"Conscious auto-suggestion, made with confidence, faith, and perseverance realizes itself automatically, in all matters within reason"

Emile Coue

Think about the reasons why you should be positive. What are the positive outcomes you desire? Use the new principles that will give you confidence and hope.

Taking action is also an effective way to break negative thought or emotional patterns. If you find yourself in a negative state of mind, decide what action you can take right now to take you out of that negative emotional or mental loop, and take that action. Say something, do something, plan something. Focus on taking that action knowing it will distract the mind and help you move out of your negative or depressed mood.

Activity is the great remedy for any mental malady

Once you have found the path away from the negative thought or mindset. Stop to think and feel how you got there as this can now start to become a new path for you. You can set a new precedent. Now you know that you can drop the negative thoughts or feelings. Try to remember that path so that you can take it any time you feel dragged under by a negative thought or emotion.

You must monitor and take CHARGE of your thought life. And it STARTS with eliminating negative thoughts and replacing them with POSITIVE ONES. Master this habit and your life will immediately start to change.

Remember to never indulge any form of a victim mentality. This is OFF LIMITS and NOT ALLOWED. The habits of complaining, finding fault, and placing blame are TOXIC. They will surely rob you and others of joy, peace, and power if you choose to indulge them. Remember, you are NEVER a victim unless you choose to be. So, don't complain!!!

The universe is listening actively and carefully to your every intention, and inclination. It is always poised to say YES and to actively move you towards realizing them in your objective experience. So, immerse yourself in positive thoughts. Program your mind for positivity.

Where you direct your intention, there will also go your attention. Both conscious and subconscious. This is why you will not realize positive things if you are indulging in negative thinking.

Anticipate and expect good things to happen. Avoid the negative expectations and the dread that comes along with it. If you dread and expect negative things, you will inevitable draw them to you. Even if it is just their effect on your emotional states. Eliminate negative thoughts, words and emotions and you will create a different bias in your thinking that will now tend to produce a reality that is consistent with your new positive beliefs.

The Most Positive and Practical of Practices

Here is a challenging but highly practical practice. Accept ALL that comes to pass, all that happens to you. Yes, ACCEPT IT. ALL of it….

You may say, "why should I". Well, because it has happened. This is the PRACTICAL part of this practice. Accept it because unless you possess a time machine to go back in time and undo it. It is pointless to resist.

You must not indulge the natural tendency to judge, regret, resist, or complain about the things that have happened. Yes, even those things which you choose to label as "bad, inconvenient, or undesirable". Because complaining about and resisting the things that have come to pass is an incredibly pointless endeavor. It serves absolutely NO purpose other than to create more negative and disempowering emotions.

Think about how irrational and impractical it is to resist, judge, or complain about the things that have come to pass. This is the practice of a fool. Once a thing has happened the only obvious and logical response is to accept it as having happened. Anything other than acceptance is as futile as throwing punches at the wind. Therefore, developing the habit of moving quickly past the denial, resisting, or judging phase is a MOST practical practice.

However, this can prove to be challenging because you will be continually pulled towards judging and resisting rather than accepting it. But it is only once you have accepted it that you can then move to the POSITIVE part of the practice. And that is to determine that since it happened it is evident proof that it was necessary. That is why it has happened. Because it was necessary for it to happen. And now that it has happened it is also unavoidable. So, the next thing to do is to apply your POWER of CHOOSING to find the POSITIVE PURPOSE in it.

This is work that you must do. To direct your conscious mind to find the positive purpose in this thing that has happened. Remembering that what you focus on you find. And once you make your choice, whatever it may be, the universe and your subconscious mind says "YES". And this now becomes the course and outcome that you will experience and thus realize. So, choose to be POSITIVE.

We are quick to judge and label. As if we knew the beginning from the end. We are in the middle of our story, we may not know the next chapter, or how it will end. But, we do know it is our story and you can always write in the very next sentence.

"When things go wrong, don't go with them"
Elvis Presley

Negative thinking is a choice. You always have the power to choose a different, more positive perspective in any and every situation. Remind yourself that life is happening FOR YOU. That all the things that come your way are intended for your benefit. They are always intended to serve a positive purpose. And YOU have the privilege and the power to determine what that is.

Empowerment Habit:

Be Solution Minded

"There are no problems, only solutions"
John Lennon

I AM... Solution Minded. I know there is an answer to every question and a solution to every problem. If I seek I will find. This gives me confidence and hope.

The empowered person must possess a Solution Mindset. The certainty that to every question there is an answer, to every problem there is a solution, and to every destination there is a definite path.

There are no impenetrable roadblocks in this life. When we believe that something is not possible, it is only because we lack imagination and faith. Because there is always a way over, under, or around any challenge or obstacle that we may encounter. The answers already exist. All we must do is discover them. It is not for us to create them, but simply to find them where they already exist. To seek them out because they are already there.

This settled confidence must be one of your fundamental empowerment beliefs. That the answers to your questions and the solutions to your dilemmas already exist. They simply await your discovering them. You can now approach any and every challenging situation with this empowered mindset that the solution is already there. So, all you need to do is be willing to seek it out. Remembering that if you seek, you shall find. It is inevitable.

One effective practice for developing the habit of finding solutions to any situation is to think about it before going to sleep. Determine in your mind that there is a solution to the problem or opportunity you seek. This thought will reinforce that specific intention in your subconscious mind, and during the sleep cycle it will process to seek out the answer in the field of infinite possibility where the answer already exists. While you sleep, you activate your creative and boundless energies that will work towards moving you closer to finding the solution that is already there and waiting to be discovered.

By purposely seeding an intention into your subconscious mind, it will start to "look" for the opportunities to objectify and realize that very intention. Your powerful and mysterious super computer (subconscious mind) will be at work drawing you closer to the solution by making you more aware of the opportunities that are within your current reach at each new turn.

When you wake up, make time before you confront your daily tasks, interactions and distractions to think consciously about the solution that your subconscious mind may have set you up to discover. Write down your thoughts or insights. Make this a regular habit and you will find that it pays dividends.

When you focus on problems,
you'll have more problems.
When you focus on possibilities,
you'll have more opportunities.

What you focus on you will find

Seek to FIRST Understand The Problem:

Another practical habit of the solution minded is to, first, seek to understand any problem and dilemma that you face. Train yourself to focus NOT on trying to find solutions first. But on attempting to FIRST fully understand the issue or problem. Because when a problem is clearly understood, the possible solutions become more evident.

I know it sounds counter intuitive, but trust me, focus on understanding the problem first, before trying to solve it. Knowing that the problem and the solution are two sides of the same coin. The more clearly you understand and can articulate the problem or dilemma the clearer the solutions become. By applying this habit your problem-solving effectiveness will increase dramatically.

"Every problem contains the seed of its own solution"
Norman Vincent Peale

Empowerment Rule #7

Your
Intentionality
Determines
Your
Potentiality

"Ultimately, human intentionality is the most powerful evolutionary force on this planet"
George B. Leonard

Intention is the principal force that sets in motion the visible and invisible sequences that produce all the material outcomes and objective results we experience. To the degree that you have an intention for something is to the degree that you have the potential to realize it.

Remember the sequence introduced in rule #3:

Where there is a want, there is a will.
And where there is a will, there is a way.

All the effects that are brought about in your life are the result of your choices and actions. And your choices and actions are both the products of your conscious and subconscious intentionalities.

Therefore, you are continually producing the effects in your life by way of your own conscious and subconscious intentions which over time become manifested and experienced in some form and to some degree.

The universe uses the principles of cause and effect, of reaping and sowing to bring about and objectify any potentiality that exists in the field of infinite possibilities (more on infinite possibilities in Rule #10). Just as any physical action (cause) has a physical effect. Then it follows that any non-physical action (thought) must also have a non-physical effect. But an effect nonetheless.

This process of cause and effect of our intentions and emotion is what is continually playing out in the invisible, universal realm of thought and emotional energy. And these inevitably surface as the objective actions and material results we realize and experience.

The Universe as a Medium

Every effective medium is designed to be specifically suited for sustaining the life forms that exist in it. Our universe is therefore perfectly designed and wired for the purpose of enabling our existence. It is the medium that is purposely designed to allow us to survive and to thrive.

The survival part speaks to the biological elements that provide for our basic life functions (breathing, eating, growing, healing, etc.). This points to the physical properties of the medium. The air, water, temperature, atmosphere, available food, etc.

But, there is also the higher purpose of this medium, which is to provide us the ability to THRIVE. And how it enables us to thrive is by its ability to materialize and objectify our thoughts and intentions.

This points to the invisible, non-physical properties of the medium. The universe provides the medium by which purposeful and intentional beings can objectify (make visible and physical) their invisible intentions (thoughts and ideas). This is a very powerful and practical realization. Our world (universe) is the perfectly suited medium in which we live and can thrive in. This is the purpose for which it was designed.

The universe is the medium by which purposeful and intentional beings (humans) can realize and materialize their thoughts and intentions.

Our physical bodies interact with and navigate through this medium in a localized manner by way of our physical bodies, senses and capabilities. However, our minds interact with and navigate in this medium in a much more mysterious manner. In a non-localized way. You cannot pin point the mental activities to any particular place or exact physical location. We think and imagine beyond any physical location. Our thoughts and imaginings exist in a non-localized way.

This is because our invisible qualities and capabilities are plugged in to and are part of the invisible field of energy and potentiality that fills the entire universe. The universal field of consciousness. The infinite field of potentiality. Call it what you will. But our subconscious/conscious minds are mysteriously plugged into and connected to this invisible medium that permeates all existence.

At the heart of all that exists there is the very energy that produces and sustains it. All visible things are produced and sustained by the invisible thought-like energies that pervade all existence. It is thought energy (consciousness) continually having an effect on the invisible raw materials of the universe (quantum particles) that causes them to organize in such a way that they produce the realized, visible, physical realities that we experience.

There is only one possible source for all the visible, physical things. And that source is the invisible energy that permeates all existence. And this invisible energy is activated by our very own consciousness, by the power of our thoughts and intentions (conscious and subconscious). And this thought energy becomes magnified and amplified by the power of our emotions and our actions.

We are swimming in an invisible sea of universal energy that connects us all. This medium makes it possible for us to survive, thrive, and realize in an interconnected way with everyone else that exists in this medium. This is the mystery of our universal existence.

The universe is always engaged in a magic dance, interweaving the individual and collective intentions and actions of all conscious beings to produce the shared objective realities which we all experience. As such, it must be continually "listening" for these intentionalities. Yes, the universe is always tuned in and picking up our intentions. And once we have declared them, we are inevitably moved along in a direction that is conducive to expressing and objectifying those intentions.

It is by our intentionality that we energize ourselves and the raw materials of the invisible quantum universe. Which is always listening, waiting on consciousness to activate and define it. To "tell it" what it is to become in the outward illusion of objective materiality.

We can see all around us the things our intentions have produced. Consciously and subconsciously, individually and collectively we have all brought about this present reality. As the visible flows from the invisible following the principle of cause, (process/time), and effect.

We are the agency and the universe the medium by which the latent infinite potentialities that exist in the quantum universal field can become realized and brought forth.

Creation is complete in the sense that all possibilities exist, and the means to manifest them are always available and at work. But the full manifestation of this completed creation is an ongoing, mysterious, and wonderful process. And we all have the privilege to be part of it.

We are all actively (wittingly or unwittingly) participating in the process of manifesting the possibilities that exist in the quantum field of infinite possibilities. This is a high privilege and responsibility. To know that we are the agency of the universe, that it is only us, humans, that can bring forth and manifest from the sea of infinite potentialities is both sobering and empowering. The universe is perfectly suited for this purpose. It is not set against us, it is holding itself out to us.

The Source of Intentionality

Where does intentionality come from? Intentionality flows from your true self. From the core of your being. From your higher self. From the deepest part of who you are. It is your intentionalities that define and reveal who you are. Your "I AM". So, it can rightly be said that I am that which I intent to be and thus become.

By being intentional we bring forth the very spirit that is within us. As our intentions reveal our innermost self. Yes, by being intentional we are demonstrating our very spirit. And our spirit is the most powerful causative agency in all the universe. The intentionalities of mankind rule the outer world. The collective spirit of mankind determines all the visible physical outcomes.

Always remember that you were designed to be a highly purposeful and intentional being. You have the capability to set your mind, by way of your imagination and creativity, on anything you want to attain, do, or experience. And it is this setting of your mind power (intentionality) that is the mysterious instigator of all things in our physical existence.

When there is a lack of purposed intention then we inevitably act in preprogrammed conditioned, and instinct driven ways. These are the lower qualities of our human nature. These are our animal like qualities, possessed by the rest of the animal kingdom.

What separates us as higher beings is our ability to be self-aware, self-conscious, purposeful, and intentional. These are the higher qualities that distinguish us from the rest of the created order. And it is in our proper and consistent application of these higher qualities that we live up to our birthright and rightly stand out and apart from the rest of the created beings. Remember, we are the crowning jewel of all creation.

Intentionality Versus Instinct and Conditioning

Animals are ruled almost entirely by instinct and conditioning. Human beings also possess instinct and over time develop many conditioned responses (as we have covered previously). But what truly separates us from the rest of the created order is that we have the ability to be purposeful and intentional. We can set and direct our intentions on anything we purposely determine. And on things that are beyond just our basic survival. We can be intentional for higher, nobler, and more lofty purposes.

When we act out of instinct or conditioned responses we express our animal qualities. However, when we act in purposeful, intentional ways we express our higher, divine qualities. It is our self-awareness and intentionalities that define us collectively and as individuals

We are meant to be purposeful and intentional beings. However, sadly, the pressures, frustrations, and mundane activities of this daily life scatters our attention and our intentions. We therefore often tend to act and display reactionary and conditioned patterns of behavior rather than purposeful and intentional actions. This diffuses our effectiveness and compromises our empowerment.

How do you set your intentionality?

You must declare it in your mind. Set it clearly and definitively in your thoughts. "I want this", "I desire this". State your intentionalities for things, goals, experiences, outcomes, etc. Be clear and honest with yourself in every area of your life (work, relationships, self).

If you want a certain thing to be certain way. Declare it. Make it known to you. If you want to accomplish or experience specific things, then you must be clear within yourself. You must plant these thoughts as your desired intentionalities. Intention is the directed and attended thought or thought energy that becomes the precursor to manifesting any outcome or result.

Our intentionalities are brought about by our persistent thoughts and beliefs. It is our attention that sets and settles our intentions. We must continually place our attention on the intentions we most want to manifest. It is by way of our intention and attention that we can bring forth those realities from the infinite, invisible sea of possibilities that is the backdrop of our existence.

An attended thought, a thought persisted in.
This is intentionality.

A fleeting thought has little to no power to materialize. Conversely, specific and persistent thoughts (intentions) have great power and potential for manifesting in the objective reality.

Remember that our thoughts are the seeds that contain their latent potential, but it is not until there is a specific intentionality that the thought becomes "planted" in the fertile environment of the invisible quantum field of consciousness. Where it can now become an effective cause that energizes the medium it is planted in to produce effects corresponding with that thought intentionality.

So, picture our intentions as taking any specific thought and planting it in the ground (our attention) where it now can begin to realize its potential.

A seed, prior to being placed in the ground only possesses a latent potential to create its corresponding effect (tree, plant, etc.). But once placed in the fertile soil, magic starts to happen. Once planted, that latent potential becomes active, powerful, and effective. It will now produce a wonderful material effect of its own kind. This is how we must view our intentionality.

How is it that we declare an intention that is picked up by the listening universe? Just how is it that we can "plant" an intentionality that can become an effective cause in our lives capable of producing its corresponding effect?

This process can be compared to the physical process of reaping and sowing. And can be stated like this:

Your Intentions...are the seeds
Your Attention...is the soil
Your Emotions...are the sunlight
Your Actions...are the water

These work together over time. And, to the degree that you persist in this process, the universe then yields the corresponding result. Which is **the fruit of this process**. The universe must produce an objective result, because this is what it is designed to do. Just like the ground will yield its crop in its due season.

Intention + Attention + Emotion + Action =
Objective Physical Effects

You see, you not only "plant the seed of potentiality" in your own mind. But since your mind is connected to the invisible field of consciousness that permeates all creation, you have also planted that seed of intentionality in the medium of the universe. And the universe is always listening, and always actively working to realize the intentions of purposeful beings. To objectify our purposes and intents.

As we have intentions we cause a ripple in the very fabric of existence. This ripple can be nurtured and magnified by way of our attention, directed emotion, and dedicated actions. And as it grows, the ripple becomes a wave that brings to bear an effect on the actual material stuff of the physical universe and thus produces the objective realities we experience outwardly.

These ripples of invisible intentionalities become concrete and manifest as visible, physical realities as things or situations. We realize and manifest our intentionalities to the degree that we persist in them over time. When you set your clear intentions, it beckons that very thing to come forth as a more viable possibility from the sea of infinite potentiality.

The Values of Potentiality

We have infinite potential, there is always a level of probability for us to be able to achieve anything at all. The potential is there, because it already exists in the field of infinite potentiality (see rule #10). We have the free choice to move towards any of the infinite doors of possibility that exist. To make our way closer, and ultimately open and step through any particular door of possibility.

Yes, for all of us every potentiality exists. The potential for you to be president of the united states, to walk on the moon, to win the lottery all exist in the field of infinite potentiality. They all exist. The variable is the percentage of likelihood. Some things are very likely, while others very unlikely. But all possible nonetheless.

The value of potentiality for anything can NEVER be zero. Because we exist in a field of infinite potentiality and therefore, for ANY possibility, there is always SOME level of potentiality, however large, or however small. Even if it is near zero, there still exists a potentiality and therefore always a possibility. You can say it this way:

**Anything at all that can happen,
may, and could happen.**

If there was a way to calculate the probability of any eventuality, we could theoretically put an actual number on it. Let's use a hypothetical example; if you were currently employed in the local fire department, your potential to become the fire chief may be, let's say, 40%. But for someone else that is not currently in the fire department or has no prior experience in that field, their potential to become the fire chief may be 3%, or 1%, or .2%. We do not know the actual value of potentiality. But the point is that there is ALWAYS a value of potentiality.

If your intentionality is to never swim in an ocean, you will naturally have a lower potential to swim in an ocean. But keep in mind that while your potential for swimming in an ocean may be very low, since you do not have the intention to do so, it will never be ZERO. As you may accidentally fall in, someone may purposely push you in, or some other "unexpected" event may cause you to be swimming in an ocean. The possibility for that eventuality is always there.

This illustrates the dynamic and unpredictable nature of our existence. Simply because you do not have the intention for something does not mean that it may not still happen. As the potential for anything to happen can NEVER be zero. The potential for anything is always there. Because we exist in a quantum universe where infinite possibilities all exist in the field of infinite potentiality. The potential for anything can never be and will never be zeroed out.

Therefore, truth we must accept is that since our potential for achieving ANYTHING is NEVER ZERO, we can never legitimately use the excuse that "this can never happen". If we quit it is not because we can't achieve it, it is because we choose not to pursue it. Or have decided that it is not worth our efforts over time. Remember, it is never that we can't. It is that we don't.

"Winners never quit, quitters never win"

I am reminded of a scene from the classic comedy "Dumb and Dumber". Where Lloyd asks his love interest Mary, "What do you think the chances are, of a guy like you and a girl like me ending up together" She responds by saying "Not good" to which he then asks, "You mean, not good like one out of a hundred?" She replies, "I'd say, more like one out of a million." He thinks briefly about her answer and then responds with the punch line. "So, you are telling me there is a chance, YEAH !!!!"

While his response may at first seem silly, funny, and unreasonable. He responded in an empowered way. Because the truth is that there was a possibility. However unlikely or improbable, there was a possibility nonetheless. The empowered truth is that if Lloyd were to continue in his intentionality to "end up" with Mary in creative, active, and persistent ways, he would progressively increase his potential to one day "end up" together with Mary. It could happen.

Therefore, we can never say, never (this is the classic cognitive dissonance phrase). In every situation, we are always faced with a decision. How badly do we want the particular thing? How unrealistic and unreasonable do we choose to become in order to improve our potentiality and increase our probabilities over time of achieving any of our desires or objectives.

How Your Intentionality Increases Your Potentiality

As your intentionality increases, so does the potential for that thing to be realized. As the potential for a thing to happen is directly proportional to the intentions for that thing to happen. It is intentionality that draws one towards the thing intended and increases the potential for it to become manifested or realized. This is an important and empowered understanding of potentiality and possibilities.

If you do not play the violin, the chances of you becoming a famous world class violin player are very, very low, maybe one in 100 billion. But today you decide that you want to become a world class violin player. Because of this intentionality your potential has now immediately increased. Your chances may now be one in 200 million. Your intentionality now produces dedicated action, and you go out and buy a violin and you start learning how to play it. Now your potential increases to one in 100 million.

The more you practice and stay on your intentional path the more you start to draw that possibility closer and closer as you continually increase your potential. Your potentiality meter will continue to move UP. As you persist with intention, attention, and actions you will continually increase your potentiality to realize that intention.

Keep in mind that in the process there will be objective and collective effects of your dedicated actions. And as you get closer you also become affected by the intentions of others along similar paths of intention. However, the point is that there is **the potential and the path** for you to one day become a world class violinist. If you quit, then the potential meter reads statistically very low. However, as we persist, we move the needle higher and create a greater and greater possibility for that outcome to become realized.

As your intention towards any specific thing grows, so does your potential for realizing that very thing. As intention and potential are directly proportional. The higher the intention the higher the potential.

Low intentionality = Low potentiality

High intentionality = High potentiality

If your intention is to love your wife, you will have a greater potential to love your wife.

If your intention is to succeed at your work, you will have a greater potential to succeed at your work.

If your intention is to be healthier, you will have a greater potential to be healthier.

If your intention is to lose weight, you will have a greater potential to lose weight.

If your intention is to be more patient, you will have a greater potential to be more patient.

What are your intentions????
Remember, they will determine your potential.

The encouraging, empowering realization is that the very instant we set our intentionality on any possibility we desire to realize, our value of potentiality increases instantly and dramatically. And it will continue to rise to the degree that we remain intentional. It is our intentionality that opens the pathway and shines a light in the direction of realizing that intention. It can be said that your intentions magnetize you towards their realization. You are then, by way of your imagination, emotions, and actions drawn along closer and closer to realizing and experiencing the objective reality of your intentions. Yes, you will eventually realize the object of your intention. If you stay on that path.

So, set your intentions to increase your potential. And as you persist in your intentions and back them with consistent actions their realization is inevitable…assuming you are patient and persistent.

At some point you may ask, "but there are many things in my life that I am certain I did not intend. So, if I did not directly intend this thing then how did it come to pass?"

Well, there are **three** primary points to consider in response to this:

First: Many of our intentions are brought about by way of our subconscious programming. Therefore, we may not always see the connection between our intention and the outcome or situation.

Second: As stated before, our intentionalities play out over the course of time. As such, we may not be aware that we are in fact reaping the results of prior intentionalities. As they are often separated by a significant amount of time.

Third: We are also exposed to experiencing objective realities that are brought about by others that we interact with, both directly and indirectly. As the Universe is continually interweaving the subconscious and conscious intentions, emotions, and actions of all people to produce the outward objective realities that we collectively experience.

However, we must always be reminded that no matter what specific situation or outcome the outside collective intentions may bring our way, each of us still have the power of our own sovereign agency. To receive, perceive, and respond to any situation in any way that we choose.

We have the power to choose our responses and furthermore, to assign meaning and purpose to every event and circumstance we experience. So, no matter what situation we find ourselves in, there is still that **most excellent power of choice.**

We are never at the mercy of any outside situation. We are only ever at the mercy of our own choices of thoughts, intentions, and actions. We can never be truly victimized by outside influences or the effects of the collective intentions. It is only ever by our own mindset and choices that we can believe ourselves to be downtrodden, defeated, or victimized.

"A particular train of thought persisted in,
be it good or bad, cannot fail to produce its
results on the character and circumstances.
A man cannot directly choose his circumstances,
but he can choose his thoughts,
and so, indirectly, yet surely,
shape his circumstances"
James Allen

There is a greater wisdom inherent in this universal one mind. This collective field of consciousness and infinite possibilities. As it often brings us, not necessarily or directly what we want, but more accurately, what we truly need in order for us to achieve what we want.

As we covered in Rule #5, we must choose to see obstacles, NOT as things that get in our way. But embrace them as the necessary means by which we can move closer to realizing our intentions. They provide us the necessary lessons and experiences we most need for our growth and betterment. In order to move towards realizing those very things we intend and desire.

"You can't always get what you want,
but if you try some time, you find,
you get what you need"
Mick Jagger/Keith Richards

The empowered way to understand this is that you do not necessarily always get what you want. But, you ALWAYS get what you need, in order to be able to get what you want. Do you see this?

I AM... I CAN...

Another way to state that intentionality determines your potentiality is by using the Empowerment Phrase "I AM... I CAN...."

I AM, is the intentionality. It is what you purpose to BE. Whatever you associate with your **I AM** is what you are, and thus will determine the very things you have the potential for. **I CAN**, is the potentiality. Because I can do those things that I purpose and intend to do.

I AM Strong. Therefore, I CAN bear a heavy burden.

I AM kind. Therefore, I CAN offer love and courtesy to others.

I AM smart. Therefore, I CAN understand things.

I AM loving. Therefore, I CAN offer love to others.

I AM successful. Therefore, I CAN find ways to succeed.

Whatever you place after the I AM, you associate with who you are and will thus inevitably define you to some degree. So, be mindful of what qualities or concepts you consciously associate with I AM.

Your "I AM" defines, limits, and, ultimately determines the sum of your potentiality. However, you can choose to alter and magnify your potentiality. But only to the extent that you are willing to modify, extend, and magnify your thoughts, ideas, beliefs, desires, emotions, words, and actions. Therefore, change your I AM. So, as you change or modify your I AM, you change and modify your I CAN.

Our intentionality is at the heart of who we are and desire to be. A mindset may be shaped unintentionally. It is called negative unconscious programming. But when we are purposeful and intentional in shaping our mindsets, that is when our empowerment truly begins to happen.

So, here is the process... Intention sets your attention, which inspires your emotions, which feed your desires, which prompt the actions, that produce the results. Therefore, to be master of self, your intentions must precede mindset. Then your mindset is formed from your intentions which come from your true source. Your I AM. Your true self, Your Empowered Self.

You have the power to choose and the universe is at your beckoning, poised and ready to realize and materialize the very substance of your intentions. It is in the persistent pursuit of your intentional wants that you become who you are purposed and destined to be. When you act out of your purposed intentions you reveal your true Empowered Self, your true I AM.

Empowerment Habit:

Be Purposeful and Intentional

"The purpose of life is to live a life of purpose"
Richard Leider

I AM…purposeful and intentional. I know that my intentionality determines my potentiality. Those things I intend I will realize. When I bring a purposeful, intentional attitude to all situations this then enables me to live up to my highest potential.

To live a truly empowered life you must be clear about your intentions in every area of your life. Because it is your intentions and attention that are the initiators and instigators of all the potential outcomes you desire.

The product of your life is the fruit of your intentionality

We must be intentional, not just on the big things like what career you want to pursue, what major life goals you want to attain, etc. But also, in the small things like; How do I want this conversation or interaction to play out? What effect do I want this email to have? How do I want this evening to be as I am home with my family? Etc. Not wishful thinking but clear, intentional mind attitudes.

Make it a habitual practice to be present in the moment and intentional in your thoughts. Develop the habit of keeping the things that are important to you, those things you want to have or achieve as front of mind. Dig them up from the floor of your consciousness and lift them up to center stage. Elevate them, as these are YOUR desires and intentions. They are supposed to be at the heart of your thinking, attention, and active consideration.

The empowered individual makes it a habitual practice to set clear intentions in the 3 key areas of life: **Work-relationships-self.** Being clear within yourself about your primary intentions in each of these areas is key to having the greater potential to realize them.

Keep an active mental (and written) record of your highest intentions in each of these three areas of your life. Because when you think more purposely, you become more intentional and thus will bring forth greater power and effectiveness of achievement.

Take the time to clearly define and settle on your intentional desires. While this may sound obvious, it is not always practiced. For instance, if you desire to be successful at work, then you must be clear and consistent in setting that intention. Acknowledge it on a regular basis and make sure to take steps towards that intention as often as they become apparent and available. You must move in the direction of your intentions anytime and every time you perceive the opportunity to do so.

If you do not enjoy arguing with your son/daughter. Then set your intentionality that you do not want to argue with them. If you do not want to get angry or upset at your husband/wife, then set your intention that you do not want this. If you want to become healthier and more fit, then set an intentionality to do so, etc.

As you become more practiced at being intentional in every area of your life this sets in motion your potentiality to realize those very things. And, since you are clearer in your intentions you will inevitably see greater opportunities to realize them, because what you focus on you find.

Your intentions are your settled wants. Remember that your power is in your wants, as this is what energizes you to take the mental and physical actions that move you in the direction of realizing and materializing these wants.

Continually List Your Intentions in the 3 Key Areas of Life:

Relationships / Work / Self

Relationships:

I want to…
Love and desire my husband/wife
Have a positive relationship with my Mother/Father.
Have a more fulfilled relationship with my children.
Be more complimentary to all people
Meet more people and make more friends
Seek out my perfect partner…etc.

Work:

I want to…
Be highly successful at work.
Be inclined to do more than expected so I can keep succeeding.
Be more positive and proficient.
Be extra helpful to my customers.
Be extra supportive of my team mates.
Be more willing to volunteer on projects
Develop my own business… etc.

Self:

I want to…
Eat better, Exercise more.
Maintain better posture.
Read more books that will help me grow
Learn another language.
Travel to Hawaii
Be more patient… etc.

It is up to you to fill in your intentionalities in the three areas listed above. From the big things to the little things. The point is to become more practiced and proficient at living with greater purpose and intentionality in every area of your life. As this sets the stage for greater achievement and fulfillment.

By actively stating your intentions clearly and consistently you cut through the ambiguity that often besets us. You now have set a clearer path. This path of intentionality becomes a roadmap for your subconscious and conscious attention to travel by as they initiate the subsequent energies, both physical and invisible, that propel you down the path that will lead to objectifying your intentions more and more.

Remember that clarity leads to singularity. The clearer you are the nearer you are. Magical and mysterious things will happen as you become more intentional and therefore clearer. Not only have you now become more inclined and open to realizing those intentions, but the universe will conspire on your behalf to also draw you nearer to that potential reality that your intentions have energized in the field of infinite possibility.

You will find that intentions not only work from the inside out but also from the outside in. Because it will seem like the universe, now knowing your intentions, will continually offer up opportunities for you to realize those intentions.

Since you now have clearly stated intentions, your subconscious mind will also be tuned in to the many opportunities that always exist for you to act on and realize those very intentions. It will be as if you are now magnetized to finding those external opportunities that will lead to realizing those very things you intend.

Be a Goal Setter and Goal Getter

A goal is a very clear, concrete, and specific intention. Intentions are powerful as they determine your potential. Goals are hyper charged intentions. As they make your intention very clear and objective. They are intentions with a bigger carrot.

Goals are important as they provide you a clear point of convergence. Without goals, we simply kick the ball around pointlessly and with no sense of purpose. However, once you establish a clear goal post now there is a definite purpose and clarity around how we direct our efforts. The goal post makes the intention super clear….to SCORE.

Setting and achieving goals is very empowering.

Goals Empower you. They give you something to chase and therefore fill you with the hope of achievement thus positioning you to demonstrate your power. A goal is a choice to realize something that is not yet real in your life. It is by your goal setting that you position yourself to become a positive attainment machine.

"What you get by achieving your goals is not as important as what you become by achieving your goals"
Henry David Thoreau

Difference Between a Wish and a Goal

A wish is something that you hope will somehow, sometime, someway come to you. A wish is disconnected from the reality of cause and effect. As you expect it to descend on you like a dove, out of nowhere for no reason. A wish is a mirage. There is no real connection to objective reality. So, don't make a wish.... set a goal.

A goal is something you intentionally and persistently drive towards. You know it can be yours and all you have to do is align all your faculties in the direction of that goal and it will be realized over time.

"A wish is a deception. A goal is an inspiration."

Think of any sport, the goal line is very obvious, and the athlete is continually driving and stretching to attain it. Whether it is to pass the goal line, sink the basket, clear the hurdle, etc.... Setting goals is a form of visualizing. You are visualizing the end result, the outcome. Developing strong habits of CLEARLY visualizing your end results in every area of your life is a very important empowerment habit. As you visualize the end result you can see them more clearly which means that you are getting closer to realizing them. Because it is a fundamental truth that...

"The clearer you are, the nearer you are"

Therefore, set goals with SPECIFIC dates, timelines, amounts, outcomes, etc. What you want to achieve, by when, how much, in what manner, with what specific end result, etc. The more specific you can be when setting goals, the more powerfully you direct the flow of the creative energies towards manifesting that specific intention. This form of specific, clearly visualized goal setting is like developing any other skill. The more you do it the better you become.

So, set your intentionality to become a visionary goal setter. Start the practice of making notes of your goals. From the broad and vague to the specific and detailed. Clear goal setting and results visualization like any skill, will develop over time. In developing this skill, you will become more empowered in making your potentialities into realities more and more. You will become a more practiced and expert creator of your objective world.

Achieving the goal is the convergence point between the intent and the realization. It is the magic point where the universe confirms the desire and validates the process flow from intent to physical reality. This is what the universe is wired to do. To make the invisible internationalities manifest in the outer objective, empirical world.

The Power of Stating Your Intention

There is great power in formally stating your intentions. In any situation, what is your intention? State it. This cuts through the ambiguity and makes YOU clearer. This clarity will cause you to act in ways more consistent and aligned with your stated intention.

In a business meeting, group gathering, or family occasion, it is appropriate and powerful to openly state the intention for the gathering. As, once again, this cuts through any possible ambiguity as to why the group is gathered. This sets clarity for the group intention. It is the "we are gathered here today" statement.

State publicly the purpose/intention for the gathering when starting a meeting, directing a project team, gathering with family for a special occasion, etc. State the purpose for the occasion and say a few words to affirm and honor the purpose for that gathering.

Also, develop the habit of stating your intentions to yourself when spending time with friends, family, or at work. What is my purpose here? Why am I gathered here? Acknowledge and set that purposeful intention in your own mind. As this will predispose you to making the most out of those situations whatever they may be. The more purposeful you are the more powerful you will be.

Practice and master this habit of directing your thoughts and intentions in the purposeful, positive directions that YOU want, and you will more effectively direct the outcomes in your life. Do not become discouraged as no new behavior or skill takes hold immediately. Be confident, be persistent, and you will see the gradual yet significant positive changes that this will yield in your life.

This process starts when you embrace the knowledge that it can be so, and then, the confidence that it will be so. Because it is your intention. And now you know that it is your intentionality that determines your potentiality.

Empowerment Rule #8

You Can Realize Anything You Desire, Believe And Act On

"Impossible is not a fact, it is an opinion. Impossible is not a declaration, it is a dare. Impossible is potential. Impossible is temporary"
Muhammad Ali

Now that you understand that what you focus on you find, and that your intentionality determines your potentiality, I can now introduce the empowerment rule that states: You can realize anything you desire, believe, and act on. This is the encouragement rule, because it provides the assurance that you can realize absolutely anything at all. Provided you desire it, believe it, and act on it.

The truth paradigm behind this rule is that the universe is not antagonistic towards you. It does not withhold from you. It is not resisting you. It does not deny you. On the contrary, the Universe is looking out for you. It is continually holding out before you the opportunities to realize the very things you truly intend and desire.

Remember that the universe is designed to be the medium by which conscious beings can objectify their intentions.

"When you want something, all the universe conspires in helping you to achieve it"
Paul Coelho, The Alchemist

This is a world of infinite possibilities. Anything that can be imagined can be realized and achieved. If you seek you will find, if you ask it will be given, if you knock the door will be opened. The Universe always says "YES" (Empowerment rule #10). We are the ones that deny ourselves by our limiting beliefs. And by our lack of faith, confidence, and unwillingness to act.

The Universe is always ready and willing to yield anything that you truly desire. This is what it is designed to do. It is not a passive medium. It is active and continually listening for and responding to your intentions. Always eager and willing to faithfully fulfill its purpose of being the medium by which our invisible intentions can transform into objective realities.

The universe not only receives from us, but also works independently through its own mechanisms and harkens back to us. Our intentions go forth into the Universe. They literally flow to the ends of creation in the quantum reality. And, in its infinite wisdom, the universe always works out the best way to objectify and manifest the individual and collective intentions of all conscious beings. It is always engaged in the universal, mysterious dance of weaving together the intentions that energize the invisible force that fills all existence. Causing it to ultimately produce all our collective, objective realities. Thus, continually manifesting and bringing forth the destinies of us all.

You must embrace this belief that the universe is not out to get you; that it is, in fact, looking out for you as the perfectly designed medium in which you are able to live and thrive in.

There is a principle and a process for everything. The power of principles is that they express universal, objective truths. If you follow a principle it will yield its corresponding result, as principles work and have their effect regardless of the user, or the user's knowledge of the principle. They are non-judgmental and non-discriminatory. Principles are 100% consistent and reliable. This is what qualifies them as principles.

Definitions of Principle:

"A law or fact of nature that explains how something works or why something happens. A fundamental truth or proposition that serves as the foundation for a system of belief or behavior."

When you act in accordance with the proper principles, you become an affective causative agent. And thus, can experience a more positive, productive, and empowered life. Empowerment rule #8 provides us the simple, yet powerful formula that can rightly be called the universal formula for positive achievement.

Universal Formula for Positive Achievement:

Want it + Believe It + ACT on it = Receive It

Step #1: Want it (Have a clear intention and burning desire)

Step #2: Believe it (Have Faith. Be convinced it can be yours. Clearly visualize it)

Step #3: Act On it (Commit to persistent, positive actions over time)

Step #1: Want it

"Definiteness of purpose is the starting point of all achievement"
Napoleon Hill

To accomplish or experience any specific objective in life, you must start here. You must be CLEAR and intentional about your wants, goals, and desires. This is where the process begins, with your intentionality. Because, remember, it is your intentionality that determines your potentiality. We must continually set our goals and desires clearly and firmly in our minds. Because it is our wants that energize our will. We must plant our intentions, our wants in the quantum field. This is the starting point to all achievement.

Most people have not taken the time or developed the habit of setting clear goals or objectives in their lives. They are not intentional and therefore unclear within themselves about the specific things they truly desire to have, experience, or achieve.

When you ask most people what their goals and objectives are, they cannot offer clear, thoughtful, confident answers. This is because they have not become accustomed to directed, sustained intentional thinking. They neglect setting their minds to those things they truly desire to achieve, realize, or experience. They are not living intentional and purposeful lives. Sadly, they are not living up to their highest purpose.

If you are not clear about your goals and desires, then how will they ever become real in your life? Every project needs a blueprint. To realize a dream, you must first dream. You must first plant the seeds before you can enjoy the fruit. A man or woman without clearly stated goals or purposes is very much a like ship without a rudder. Purposeless and aimless in the sea of life. Being tossed to and fro by the capricious winds and sweeping currents of life.

As we have all experienced, the winds and currents of life's circumstances can be quite formidable. Without clear goals or stated purposes, you will surely flounder and fail. You will feel frustrated, hopeless, and wonder why you can't experience success or fulfillment in the different areas of your life. You will feel like the eternal victim, rather than empowered and victorious as you are meant to be.

However, when you have clearly stated intentions, goals, and desires, you now have a roadmap that provides the needed direction pointing you forward on the path towards achievement. The clearer the roadmap, the more effectively you can navigate through or around those head winds and currents of daily life. With a clear roadmap, you have a key tool that enables you to more effectively navigate towards and ultimately arrive at your desired destination.

In addition to not having clearly stated goals and objectives, most people operate from the disempowering paradigm that says; "What is the point?" I don't have it, so that must mean I can't get it". "why bother, I will fail, I can't get that, it is not meant for me, etc.". When we indulge in these disempowering mindsets we fail before we even reach the starting line. We deny ourselves before we even begin.

We see that other people have and achieve more and better things. But we do not associate this with our own lives. Believing that what we currently have or who we currently are is all that there can be for us. We are always settling, unable to see beyond our current circumstances. Believing that this must be "as good as it gets", "the best I can do", or "all that there is for me".

Most of us are guilty of living "realistic" lives. Quietly settling for our current reality. Never realizing that what we currently have does not need to determine or limit the things we can realize in the future.

"The mass of men live lives of quiet desperation"
Henry David Thoreau

Who we currently are, or what we currently have are only the result of what we have desired, acted on, and accepted up to this point. It does not need to be the predictor of future events. We must not let what we currently see determine who, or what we will continue to be.

You must be willing to see past your current circumstances. Understanding that current circumstances are only the product of the past. Current situations are only the effect of our prior causations. The future is not yet determined, and you have the power to choose different. And in choosing different you can become different and realize the different, better things you desire. To make any change in your life, you must first change your mind.

"Our Current situation does not determine how far we go, only where we begin"

If you really want it, YES, you can really have it. If you believe that you can't then you can't, but if you believe that you can, then you can. The answer is always "YES" (Empowerment Rule #10).

To achieve and realize your goals and desires you must first allow yourself to want, to desire. You must NOT deny yourself. You must have the settled confidence that if you want something, it can be yours. The universe does not hold back. It does not deny us; we deny ourselves by not asking or not allowing our desires to be expressed, embraced, and acted on.

The universe is not out to get you, it is looking out for you. There is a principle and a process for achieving all things. There is a path leading to any place we choose. All we need is a desire to go, a map to get us there, and the willingness to travel.

Step ONE is to get to the place where you say, "I can have it, if I want it. I allow myself to believe and embrace that this goal or desire is something that is possible for me. Why not me, why not here, why not now?"

Once you have made this mental leap, then step one is accomplished. You have managed to get out of your own way. And now the path towards your goal is clear of its SINGLE biggest obstacle…. YOU!!! Remember rule #1 Only YOU stand in the way of YOU.

Being clear about your wants and desires is the first step to positive accomplishment. You must have clear and definite intentions. Because it is your intentionality that determines your potentiality.

"The man who wins is the one who thinks he can"
Henry Ford

You must be confident that you are fully capable of realizing anything you desire in your life. Because you have the power of choosing and the ability to act. The universe provides us the medium through which by persistent application of certain principles and processes we can realize any intentions of our minds and hearts.

The encouraging truth is that there is always a principle and a process to making any desire or goal happen. The reality is that we do not have, first, because we do not ask. And second, when we do ask, we do not ask in faith, believing it can be ours.

So, if we do not ask, and when we do ask, we do NOT believe, does it surprise us that we do NOT receive? If we do not ask, and don't believe we can get it, it will NEVER be ours.

Let's be completely honest, for many of us, the following statements apply: I don't have it because…

I have not been clear that I truly want it.
I have not desired it with intensity.
I have not asked or asked persistently.
I am not confident that it can be mine.
I do not feel worthy of it.
I do not believe I can get it.
I don't want it bad enough.

You must first give yourself permission to open the door of your imagination and confidently entertain all those things you would like to have and experience. Because all attainment starts in our minds.

"We must possess it in our mind before we will ever possess it in time"

When you want something, the first step is to focus on the WHAT. To be very clear and convinced of the specific thing or result you want. We often deny ourselves from wanting or desiring something because our default thinking tells us that since we do not currently have it, we will likely never get it.

You must be practiced at developing strong wants. Not wishful thinking, but clear, intentional, settled goals, desires, and expectations. Not denying or limiting yourself. This is where the fundamental "work" comes in. You must work on really wanting it. Remember from Rule #3: The "WANT" always comes before the "WILL". It is your "want" that activates and energizes your "WILL".

"Where there is a WANT there is a WILL. And where there is a WILL there is a WAY."

You must first work yourself to the point where your wants become settled certainties. This may seem simple, but this is where most people FAIL. They don't have it because they do not want it bad enough. Or they believe they can't get it, so they immediately deny themselves. If you were totally certain that you could achieve or realize anything you desired, what things would you desire?

Go ahead, dream. Make a list. The Universe says "YES". It does not withhold from you. It will conspire on your behalf. It is the medium that is waiting to produce the effects of your intentional choosing. It is the ocean of possibility and potentiality that is patiently and eternally waiting for you to activate it by way of your conscious intentions and subconscious energies.

The universe looks on proudly at all the things that are realized and accomplished. It celebrates every one of our achievements. As they stand as a clear testimony to the power of human intentions and the effectiveness and faithfulness of the universe as the medium to produce them. A wonderful and powerful partnership.

Continually remind yourself that it is ok to want or desire ANYTHING at all. As it is your sovereign, individual right to choose the things you want for yourself in this life. You have the power of choosing to want for yourself ANYTHING AT ALL. Know this truth, bury it deep inside of you, so it is always there to activate your power to choose.

Now you possess the certainty that as long as you are faithful to this principle of achievement anything that you want, CAN, WILL, and MUST be yours.

Life is your candy store and you can have any candy you desire. Do not restrain yourself because of self-imposed limitations. Go for the biggest candy bar in the store. It's ok, you can have that one if you want it. This is an empowering mindset and attitude.

We have not because we ask not….and when we do ask, we do not mix it with faith…which is the next step.

Step #2: Believe it

"You are never given a wish without also being given the power to make it come true"
Richard Bach

Once you have a specific desire or goal firmly and persistently set in your mind, the next step is to assume the total confidence that it can and will be yours. That you are deserving of it. And that you are deserving simply because you **desire it** with deep intentionality. You must embrace the certainty that it is your right and your destiny to realize it. That's it. Believe that it is yours to achieve simply because you have been given the desire for it.

Believe and trust that the universe does not withhold it from you. To the contrary, it is holding all possibilities out to you. It is only you that can withhold it from yourself by your limiting and disempowering mindsets. Allow yourself to fully TRUST that it can be and will be yours. You must combine your desire with ABSOLUTE FAITH. Getting to this point of settled certainty, of having total Faith is the magic step.

"And all things, whatsoever ye shall ask in prayer, believing, ye shall receive."
Matthew 21:22

One way to think about your level of faith and certainty is to examine your language when you are in a state of desiring.

You must go from:
"It would be nice to have", "Sure would like to have this thing"
To the more confident state:
"I am going to get this thing", "I have got to get this thing. This thing will be mine."
To the settled, certain state of total Faith where you say:
"I GOT THIS!!! This IS mine."

This is the stage where you have taken possession of it in your mind by means of your imagination and faith. All achievement begins in the mind. We must possess it in our mind before we will possess it in time.

"Faith is the assurance of things hoped for, the evidence of things not seen"
Hebrews11:1

Think about this statement, "Faith is the evidence of things not seen". Did you ever realize that your faith is EVIDENCE? Yes, it is your faith that serves as the surety of the thing yet to be realized. Because if you have Faith, you already possess the evidence that it can become real for you. And it should be this settled faith that provides you the confidence (which literally means, "with faith", con-fidence.) that having evidence produces. This confidence (with faith) becomes the fuel that will ignite your emotions and energize you to take the positive and persistent actions that will result in realizing any of your yet to be realized, desired outcomes.

Faith and Imagination

Faith is the key that unlocks the door that brings you into the realm of making anything possible. Faith is what moves men to achieve the unreasonable and unrealistic. It is what allows us to make the invisible, visible in our lives. To the extent that a man or woman can bring to bear extraordinary faith to the ordinary circumstances of daily life, is to the extent that they will surely realize "miracles." They will make the impossible, possible.

Again, what is faith? It is the **assurance** of things hoped for. The **evidence** of things not seen.

You first need to imagine that something is possible. You must first believe it in your imagination. Remember that your imagination is the faculty you possess by which you access the field of infinite possibilities. From imagination and faith flows the wellspring of all human creation and achievement. Faith can move mountains.

"Imagination and faith are the secrets of creation"
Neville Goddard

From your imagination and faith proceeds your intentionality. And it is your intentionality that sets into motion invisible forces that energize the quantum field of infinite potential. Remember that all possibilities exist in this field of infinite potential. And it is by way of your intentions that you begin to draw out and bring forth your invisible desires from this very field of infinite possibilities.

If you desire something that is "easy" or "near", it does not require much faith. As you can quickly realize it. For example, if you want a glass of water, you simply get up and get it. You want a new shirt. You drive to the store, pick out a shirt, and if you have the cash or the credit, you can get the new shirt. These examples are simple, easy, and near. Realizing them does not involve much faith. Because you know exactly how and what it takes to realize those simple, commonplace desires.

In these simple examples, you are clear about the principles, the path, and the process to realizing them. That is why it does not involve much faith. However, if you think about it, it is no different with anything else you may want to realize. In the sense that for every achievement or attainment there is a **principle, a path, and a process**. Where the element of faith must come in to play is when we are unable to see the path, or when we are unclear about the principles or the process involved in the attainment of that goal.

"Faith is taking the first step even when you do not see the whole staircase"
MLK Jr.

The challenge comes when we decide to achieve or experience something that we are not quite sure how to get, that we have never gotten, or that seems far away from our current reality. This is when our imagination and faith must be more effectively applied.

To the degree that a desire seems out of reach, or far away is to the degree that you must be willing to activate a greater level of your imagination and faith. Which, by the way, are faculties that you not only already possess, but that you activate all the time to one degree or another. You see, even in those simple things (like getting a drink of water) you are activating your imagination and applying some measure of faith. Because you must imagine the glass of water and believe that it is there for you in order to move towards realizing it. Do you see that? Even in this, it is our imagination and faith that is at work, enabling us to realize even our simplest, everyday desires.

"To believe in the things you can see and touch is no belief at all. But to believe in the unseen is a triumph and a blessing."
Abraham Lincoln

You must condition yourself to more effectively utilize and apply your imagination and your faith to the greater degrees as needed. For the purposes of attaining ANY goal or desire that you intend to realize or experience in your life. As it is only your imagination and faith that provide you the pathway to take you beyond the boundaries of your current reasoning and reality.

When you effectively utilize your imagination and faith, you can reach the point of becoming **UNREASONABLE & UNREALISTIC**. Being unreasonable and unrealistic, contrary to popular belief, are not negative vices. They are in fact, when rightly understood, empowering virtues.

The Empowered Definition of "Unreasonable"

"The determination that you will not accept or entertain **any reason** (or excuse) that will prevent you from achieving your intentional goals, objectives, or desires."

What is it that separates you from the things that you want that you do not currently have? What separates you from those things are the specific reasons why you do not have it. It is the reasons that separate you. So, remove the reasons and you will have it. Be willing to become unreasonable!!! Where you do not accept any reason that will prevent you from achieving your desired result. Become single minded and unreasonable. It is already yours. Nothing is preventing you. You are already on your way. You will have it in time.

"Once you have decided on a goal,
you must be UNREASONABLE about it.
Accept NO reasons that will prevent
you from achieving it"

The Empowered Definition of "Unrealistic"

"The condition of believing that you have the ability to make any currently unreal thing you desire, REAL in your life. The certainty that you possess the power to make real anything that may not be currently part of your objective reality.

Remember that your senses will continually serve to dissuade you from realizing the "unrealistic" possibilities. Because your senses are continually reminding you of the present realities which we now understand are simply the echoes of the past.

Too much reliance on the physical senses will only serve to disillusion you. To cause you to move away from your illusions (which are all attainable). To achieve and attain you must trust your imagination and your faith more than you trust in your very own physical senses.

"Faith is to believe what you do not see;
the reward of this faith is to see what you believe"
Saint Augustine

When a desire seems out of current reach you must be certain and believe that it can and will be YOURS. Even though you may not, at the current time, be aware of how or when you will realize it. The key is to stay focused on the "what" and simply trust. Stop there, take a breath. Simply desire and trust. Have faith…the rest will follow.

Do not confuse the wanting and trusting with the getting it. The "getting it" part will develop over time. As it is part of a time bound process. Where you must always keep your focus is on the "what". Do NOT let the "getting it" discourage you from the wanting and believing. Because too much focus on the "how" before you are settled on the "what" can disintegrate your faith. As you will tend to become more focused on the "realistic" things that your senses are continually offering you, rather than the "unrealistic" things which you have determined in your imagination.

Even more important than having a plan is having the vison. Because once you have the vision, the plan will become clearer as you start to move forward in faith. You must therefore have the absolute trust that the way will become clearer and clearer as you make your way forward.

Too much worrying about the "how" and you may likely become discouraged. Rather, trust and focus on the NOW. What steps can you take right now? Then simply proceed with clarity of goal and with the absolute faith that you can and will attain it in due time.

To the degree that a desire seems currently out of reach is to the degree that you must have a stronger, burning desire. And be willing to mix it with a greater faith. Practically speaking, more faith simply means to be willing to hold on to the invisible belief for a longer period of time. Or to be willing to persist through a longer series of obstacles.

Empowerment Habit:

Be Patient and Persistent

**"Good things come to those who believe,
Better things to those who are patient,
and the best things to those who don't give up"**
Unknown

I AM…Patient and Persistent. I know that all things come to pass in their due time, following their own course. I will never use time as an excuse or see it as my enemy. I will use it productively and not waste it. I will wait on it and not be impatient, I will trust it and not fear it. I will respect time, as every moment is precious and holds the promise of any dream or achievement. Every moment comes to us pregnant with opportunity. Time is the necessary agent that brings to pass all things. Time is my friend. I will make the most of my time by being intentional and action oriented.

Time is often a key stumbling block for us in the pursuit of our desires. We tend to be too easily put off by the concern over how long it will take. This unwillingness to embrace the fact that any process involves time, is what often deflates our desires and evaporates our dreams. Since we don't have it (we don't see it), and we have little faith (even when deep down we know it can be ours). We are put off because we know it may take considerable time or effort to realize.

Things just take time. Everything in life MUST work through its corresponding process, and every process MUST work itself out through the element of TIME. So, you must be patient. You must trust that good things will come to those who wait, to those that persevere.

"Great works are performed not by strength, but by perseverance"
Samuel Johnson

All things come to us, not necessarily at our desired time, but always at the right time. When things don't happen right away just remember that it only takes thirteen hours to build a Toyota, but it takes six months to build a Rolls Royce. So be patient and stay on the path. Do not lose hope, do not lose faith. It will be yours if you simply believe and persist.

"A river cuts through rock, not because of its power, but because of its persistence"

Yes, it will take time. But guess what? You have the time. While you are alive, all you have is time. Even now you are expending this most precious commodity, time. You are investing your time every second of the day. The fact that realizing your greatest desires may take a greater investment of your time should NOT discourage you. You have the time. So, be patient. Know that it will not happen overnight, but trust that it will happen over time.

Microwave Mindset

We have become instant minded. We have adopted a "microwave mindset" where we expect near instant results. We want things to happen, change, or develop instantly. This attitude and expectation is disempowering as it sets us up for disappointment and frustration. Having a more practical perspective on the concept of time is healthy and necessary on our empowerment journey.

It is interesting to note that when it comes to wanting to achieve we tend to be impatient and unwilling to wait for time to yield its outcome. However, when we experience frustration, heartache, or disappointment, even if for a short time, it feels like an eternity.

You must take a more balanced perspective when it comes to time. Knowing that when desiring an outcome, it will take time and you should be patient. But, when in the process of dealing with heartache and disappointment you can take solace in the powerful adage that says, "This too shall pass".

Time heals all wounds. Over the course of time doors open, opportunities appear, perspective is gained, and wisdom is accumulated. Time will always yield its result. Trust that everything has its designated timeline and process. That all things must work themselves out by way of the arrow of time. Make friends with time.

Be patient but be persistent. Once you have decided on a goal do not be discouraged by the element of time. Convince yourself that all you must do is stay on that path. Stay in pursuit. Keep on moving in your desired direction. Trust in the power of perseverance. If you persevere you will succeed.

***"There is no substitute for persistence.
The person who makes persistence his watch-word,
discovers that "Old Man Failure"
finally becomes tired and makes his departure.
Failure cannot cope with persistence."***
Napoleon Hill

Keep the faith that as long as you stay on that road, you will get to that destination. You will realize that outcome. And when you do, it will be worthwhile and wonderful. Program yourself to not become discouraged by the element of time when it comes to realizing your desires. Stay focused, stay committed, and stay on the path. You will eventually arrive, if you stay the course.

While we must be persistent in order to achieve, we must also be FLEXIBLE. Because while the principles are few, the processes are many and varied. So, we must be patient and we must be flexible. Always remembering that inflexibility leads to breakability. But flexibility leads to invincibility. So, go with the flow.

"Stay committed to your decisions, but stay flexible in your approach"
Tony Robbins

Be patient…. "Make haste slowly" but confidently and persistently. Your achievement is certain. You have the evidence. The evidence is your faith. And your faith should breed patience and persistence because the thing is certain. All you need to do now is to ACT!!!

Step #3. Act on It

"The distance between dreams and reality is called action"

Once you have clarity about your goals and desires. Combined with the confidence and certainty that your faith provides. You can now start to make your way towards realizing them. You can now proceed with the settled certainty that it is already a "done deal". The "getting it" has already happened in the invisible state of potentiality. You already possess it in your mind.

All you need to do is move forward with the persistent actions that will bring you closer to realizing it. Towards making it real in your material, objective experience. You must act in order to see it become real and realized in your life.

Remember that you must trust it is already achieved. By applying your Imagination and faith your objective is already very real. In the invisible realm of potentiality, it is already done. So, all that you must do now is simply go GET IT. To take the actions needed to realize it, bring it forth, and experience it in your objective reality.

Now that you possess the settled certainty, you simply step forward with curious anticipation. With an attitude that says; "I wonder how it will come to pass? I am eager and patiently anxious to experience the actions and milestones that will inevitably bring me closer to this. It will be mine in time. I am certain of it"

You must now develop a positive, persistent willingness to work towards your desires. Because remember, faith without works is dead. You must take dedicated actions as often as you see an opportunity or anytime you are prompted to do so. And being that what you focus on you find, you will inevitably will find more and more opportunities to move towards those desired things that you have intentionally determined to achieve.

Let's be clear and make no mistake, it is only actions that will ultimately yield the results or outcomes you desire. It is in our actions that our faith is expressed. The wanting sets the foundation, and the believing provides the fuel. But you must use that fuel to ignite the persistent, positive actions that will ultimately serve to accomplish your goals or purposes.

Empowerment Habit:

Be Action Oriented

"When action is our priority, vanity falls away"
Ryan Holliday

I AM…Action Oriented. I understand that taking actions is the only way to manifest any desired outcome. It is only by way of dedicated and persistent actions that my intentions will become realized.

In the pursuit of any goal or desire you must always be ready and willing to persistently act. To move, to think, to plan, to speak, to respond, to initiate, to iterate., etc. In order to continually and progressively move you from the state of potentiality to the state of objective reality. Knowing that this process of achievement involves a series of dedicated actions over a period of time.

"Action is the foundational key to all success"
Pablo Picasso

There is a time for thinking and there is a time for action. While we know that developing the right mindsets is crucial to living an empowered life, we also know that action is needed to objectify our thoughts and ideals.

"What we plant in the soil of contemplation,
we shall reap in the harvest of action"
Meister Eckhart

Therefore, you must always be willing and disposed to taking empowered and practical ACTIONS in every area of your life. As part of your empowerment journey you must become practiced in right thinking that leads to right action. You must be eager to always take ACTION. The end result should always be ACTION.

"Do you want to know who you are?
Don't ask. Act!
Action will delineate and define you"
Thomas Jefferson

The Gordian Knot:

A great story to illustrate the action-oriented mindset is the Greek legend of Alexander the Great and the Gordian knot.

The story is told of Gordius, a poor peasant who arrived with his wife at the city of Phrygia in an ox cart. It had been prophesied by an Oracle that the future king of Phrygia would one day come into the city riding in a wagon. The people, seeing Gordius arrive in the ox cart decided to make him king of Phrygia.

Out of gratitude, Gordius dedicated his oxcart to the god Zeus, and tied it up to a post in the city square using a very complicated knot whose ends were tucked away within the knot.

The Oracle foretold that anyone who could untie this "Gordian Knot" would become ruler over all of Asia. During the next 100 years, many came to Phrygia attempting to untie the famed Gordian Knot, but all failed.

One day, the young and undefeated conqueror, Alexander the Great, came to the city determined to solve the mystery of the Gordian Knot. As the story goes, after many failed attempts to untie it, Alexander became frustrated, when suddenly and abruptly he stepped back declaring "What does it matter how I loosen it".

He then confidently drew his sword, raised it above his head, and with one mighty stroke, sliced the Gordian knot in half. That was the end of the Gordian Knot dilemma.

Alexander solved the perplexing problem by taking decisive action. You can argue whether he solved it the right way or not, but there is no denying that the problem was solved. There was no more Gordian Knot. Because he took immediate, decisive action. Literally cutting away the dilemma.

We can use this as an allegory in our own lives and apply it to any perplexing, persistent issue or dilemma that we may be facing. If we are frozen by fear, insecurity, frustration or any other obstacle, we must also confidently stand up, step back and declare to take immediate, decisive action. We must always be willing to ACT!!!

You must become aware of any "Gordian Knot" situations in your life. And trust that what is called for to unloose it is some form of intentional and decisive ACTION.

"Action expresses priorities"
Mahatma Ghandi

Problem Solving in Two Simple Steps:

The simplest formula for problem solving is a two-step process:

One: Honestly define the problem/opportunity

Two: Determine what immediate action can be taken to resolve it.

Say to yourself; "This is the problem, and this is what I can do right now to fix it." Then promptly take that action.

If that does not resolve the issue, that's ok, simply take the next logical step. Then the next step, and so on. If the initial action does not fully resolve the issue or concern, do not stop. Instead, wash rinse…repeat…

Keep identifying the issue and determining what actions you can take next to remedy it. As you keep taking intentional, positive actions you will inevitably move closer to your solutions and towards defining your successes.

Action is the only antidote for resolving any situation that has come about.

If you are facing challenges or issues at work, decide what actions you can take right now to move in a direction that will resolve the frustration or issue….and take those actions.

If you are concerned about a situation in your family relations, decide on what action you feel will help alleviate the situation and take that action now. If you are experiencing other relationship issues, determine what action can be taken right now to help resolve it. And take that action.

If you are frustrated about your weight or other personal issues, same thing, what actions can be taken NOW to help resolve the issue or move you forward to your stated goals or intentions. Apply this pattern to every area of your life. What can I do RIGHT NOW…What can I do NEXT? Then, DO IT!!!

You must be committed to continually taking baby steps, or bold steps in EVERY area of your life. It matters not whether those steps will magically undo the Gordian knot, but simply trust that it will move you closer to the answer or resolution that you seek. It is ultimately Action that is needed to resolve any issue or achieve any goal, whatever it may be.

Additionally, busying your hands by taking dedicated actions is an effective means in helping to alleviate any mental stress. As the commitment to action will re-focus and re-direct your energy away from any mental stress, anxiety, or frustration you may be experiencing about a situation.

Taking action is also an effective way to break negative thought or emotional patterns. If you find yourself in a negative state of mind, decide what action you can take right now to take you out of that negative emotional or mental loop, and take that action. Say something, do something, plan something. Focus on taking that action knowing it will distract the mind and help you move out of your negative or depressed mood. Activity is a great remedy to soothe any malady.

"Thinking will not overcome fear, but action will"
W. Clement Stone

Apply this to not only resolving issues or dilemmas, but also for attaining any goal or desire. "This is the goal, and this is what I can do now to get closer to its attainment." This is the default mindset of the empowered individual. To honestly and clearly define the issue/opportunity/goal and then determine what action can be immediately taken to move forward in a positive direction.

Apply this also to the rules presented in this book. Continually ask, what action can I commit to right here and right now in this area of my empowerment? List them, commit to them, DO them.

"There are risks and costs to action.
But they are far less than the long-range risks
of comfortable inaction"
John F. Kennedy

While physical action is needed to realize any goal, you must also be willing to initiate thought action. Thinking about the goal and about creative ways to achieve it as well as visualizing the goal and getting a clearer mental picture are important actions that must be consistently applied in the effective pursuit of any goal or change you desire.

One way to bring things closer is to visualize them. Because the clearer they are, the nearer you are. Build this skill of emotionally charged visualization that will inspire positive actions towards the realization of any desired objective.

Decide on the things you want and spend time thinking about them. Doing so you will bring forth ideas, questions, answers, etc. And you will start to slowly unravel the puzzle that will yield the answers or inspirations to move you closer to your goals and desires. By simply applying the power of your directed thought you are taking important necessary action.

Thoughts are the seed power that make manifestations possible. Remember that all we see around us are manifested thoughts. We are surrounded by materialized thoughts and ideas. The imagination is a very powerful faculty that we all possess and should harness and direct to our most positive and productive means. Therefore, make proper use of your conscious mind to become better at using your creative and imaginative faculties. Take thought ACTION.

"Your willingness to contemplate on the things you desire will allow you to discover how to manifest it"
Wayne Dyer

Obstacles Are Opportunities

In the process of taking dedicated and persistent actions towards realizing and achieving your desired goals you will undoubtedly face obstacles of many different types. Some physical, some mental, some situational, etc.

Remember from Rule #5 that you must choose to see obstacles and challenges that appear in your way, not as hindrances, but as the necessary means by which you can advance on your way to achieving your goals or arriving at your destination.

"The impediment to action advances action. What stands in the way becomes the way"
Marcus Aurelius

The obstacles that may be preventing your current actions from having their effect are there to cause you to implement new or different actions that will advance you towards your goal or destination. Therefore, always choose to see the obstacles that appear in any area of your life not as burdensome or inconvenient, but rather as necessary to further advance you towards achieving your goals and objectives.

Obstacles are not there to STOP you. They are there to enable you to keep going. They are necessary and essential to your ultimate success.

The obstacles we encounter bring us the lessons we must learn, the puzzles we must solve to achieve our objectives, whatever they may be. Those very obstacles that appear in our path must be welcomed, embraced, and appreciated as they are the means by which we learn and grow so that that we may ultimately achieve our desired results.

Knowing this to be true it should NOT surprise or upset us when the obstacles do show up. We should be expectant and ready to embrace them. They are signposts that we are getting closer to our goals. They contain within them the hidden gems that hold the answers to our success. The obstacles in our way hold the keys to us developing the better understanding, mindset, or skill needed to achieve our goals.

"Obstacles are friends and helpers….
"Each obstacle is a comrade in arms
forcing you to be better…
Og Mandino

Remember, in life you will encounter "problems", "adversities", and "challenges". Of every type and of varied sorts. They will come, of this you can be certain. And they should come, they are supposed to come. But, we must always see them as they truly are. As necessary ingredients in the recipes of our success. And by the power of our choosing we can turn them into opportunities and not stumbling blocks.

"You can either allow the obstacles
in your life to be the excuse for your failure,
or make them the reason for your success"

As stated in a prior chapter…

Life does not always give you what you want,
but it ALWAYS gives you what you NEED,
in order for you to be able to get what you want.

My Vision is My Mission

The mindset you must possess on your journey of achievement is captured in the statement below. It is "My Vision Is My Mission" Statement:

"I have set my intentionality on the goal that I desire.
I am deserving of it simply because I want it, believe I can get it,
and am willing to persistently work towards it."

"I am certain and confident that this goal is mine.
I will not allow myself to become distracted or disempowered by
negative or limiting thinking."

"I'm not concerned about what other people say, think, or believe
about my goal."

"I am not concerned with how long it will take or how many times I
may get sidetracked or knocked down."

"I don't care how hard it may seem at times.
Because I fully expect that disappointment, obstacles, frustrations,
setbacks and delays will come."

"But, I am ready for them. I am expecting them.
They will not surprise or discourage me.
I will accept them as a necessary part of the process."

"The challenges and obstacles are lessons and opportunities
to get me closer to my goal. They are there to test and to teach me."

"They will not cause me to serve them. They will serve me.
They will not be my master. I will master them."

"They will only confirm my resolve and
commitment to realizing my desires."

"No matter what happens I am still here, moving towards my vision.
Never deterred and confidently drawing nearer with every step."

"There is NO denying me this thing. It is MINE!!!!
I have become UNREASONABLE and UNREALISTIC."

"I will NOT accept any reasons that will prevent me from achieving what I have set in my mind and heart to achieve."

"I will not allow the current reality to dictate what my future reality will be."

"I have set this goal and desire as my destination and therefore, it is my certain destiny."

"My Vision is my Mission"

Price and Consequence

The universe is a bit like a Genie in Bottle. It is ready and willing to grant any desire. However, this Genie will NOT grant your desire instantly, simply by you invoking it. The universe is much more responsible than that. Think about how irresponsible it would be if life simply granted every desire instantaneously. If a ten-year-old wanted a flame thrower, and, puff, instantly they had a flame thrower. They would surely use it in an irresponsible and dangerous manner. Or how about if you wanted a million dollars and puff, you got it, but then used it to indulge every whim, fancy, and destructive vice…it would ruin you.

The universe, in its infinite wisdom, has a more responsible process in place. There are a number of different ways to express or attempt to define this process. One way to understand it is this…Everything in life has a PRICE and a CONSEQUENCE….

To everything in life there is a price and corresponding consequence. You want to achieve or obtain something, anything? Well, there is a price associated with it. Sometimes the price is obvious and clear (like the price tag on a shirt, a car, a house, etc.). But for many other things we do not know the exact price. Because it is a price that cannot be quantified. What is the price to pay for having a happy marriage? a healthy body? a successful career? etc. We cannot specifically quantify the price of those achievements, but they too have a price nonetheless. There is a price we must be willing to pay by way of our time, attention, actions, resources, etc.

Life is transactional. And, if you are willing to pay the price, the thing, the result, or accomplishment will be yours.

Not only is there a price to pay in order to obtain anything in this life. But in the process of obtaining it and once obtained, there is also a set of consequences that must be effectively dealt with. For instance, when you buy something in the store. You paid the price and now it is yours. But you must take it home, find a place for it, put it to use, take care of it, clean it, etc. There is a consequence. It is this way with everything we obtain or achieve in life.

Yes, to achieve any goal or desire there is a price and a consequence.
For a fulfilling relationship, a price and consequence.
For a healthy body, a price and consequence
For a successful career, a price and consequence
To achieve any particular goal, a price and a consequence
Etc….

This is the process that life follows (price and consequence), and it is this Formula of Positive Achievement in Empowerment Rule #8 that satisfies this process. Life is transactional, if you are willing to pay the price and effectively deal with and manage the consequences, you have earned the right to possess or experience the desired thing.

Anyone can bring change to their current circumstances and realize any goal, if they simply desire, believe, and act with purpose, passion, and persistence. Yes, any goal is yours to realize.

Have a VISION. Fuel it with PASSION.
Realize it with ACTION!!!

Be bold in your requests, believe trust and anticipate. Be willing and eager to take action whenever you are moved to do so. Create an "I want" list of all the things that you desire in every area of your life. Spend time each day reviewing it. Fill it with more clarity and more certainty. Also note what actions you are taking or could be taking in order to realize these goals.

Do you now see that there is NOTHING that can be held back from you if you faithfully apply the Formula of Positive Achievement? Apply it to any goal or desire that you want to realize.

Empowerment Rule #8 is the ENCOURAGEMENT RULE. It provides you the certainty that you can achieve anything you desire. Because it assures you that there is a clear universal principle and process for turning any of your desires into reality. This principle will work for anyonc that faithfully applies it.

Conceive, believe, achieve. The world is not out to get you. It is looking out for you. Life is not holding out on you. It is holding itself out to you. It will graciously grant you anything you desire, if you faithfully apply this Empowerment formula of Positive Achievement. The universe will yield you the desired thing. It must, it wants to, it revels in your achievement. It was designed to do just that.

The universe is NOT denying you…It is listening and eager to play its part in realizing your intentions. This is what it is purposed to do. It is designed and wired to objectify and produce the things we imagine, believe, and work towards.

Consider the breathtaking ocean of achievements that mankind has realized over the ages. These monumental accomplishments throughout time serve as a testimony to the power of intentionality of human beings. And to the willingness of the universe to make those intentions real.

Yes, history is filled with the amazing achievements of men and women from every generation. If they can achieve their dreams, then you too can achieve, even as you dream.

Empowerment Rule #9

It Is Supposed To Be Easy

"Everything is supposed to be Easy.
If it seems hard,
it is because you are doing it wrong,
or with the wrong attitude or intention."

This may be the most controversial Empowerment rule because all our lives we have been brain washed into believing that most meaningful things can only be attained by means of hard work. We place a romantic value on this notion of "struggle to achieve". We are enamored with the ideal that if something is worthwhile, it can only be achieved by means of herculean effort, through blood, sweat, and tears. That if we are not bearing down, working hard, grunting, huffing, and puffing to accomplish, then we are not realizing or achieving anything truly significant in our lives.

We hear over, and over again things like "you must be willing to work hard to achieve your goals and objectives." "nothing worthwhile is easy." "Some things are hard" "You must try harder" etc.

This controversial empowerment rule states that it is supposed to be easy. That all achievements should be produced by a persistent, positive, and easy-going flow of thought energy and resistance less actions. It does not need to seem “HARD”, as it is NOT supposed to be “HARD”. “Hard” is simply a label we are used to placing on the things we are not able to readily achieve. This is what we have programmed ourselves to believe and accept. But, all things are easily achievable when you have the right mindset, skill set, resources, and dedicate the appropriate amount of time.

Here again we are faced with the disempowering effects of negative labeling. The concepts of “easy” and “hard” are just labels that we choose to apply. Doing is doing. Effort is effort. Work is work. Whether we label something as “easy” or “hard” is really just a subjective choice. And remember that depending on how you decide to label it, it will become real for you. Because what you focus on you will find.

We are quick to call things out as hard, challenging, difficult, frustrating, tough, etc. But all we are really doing when applying these labels is projecting our own negative and disempowering attitude on the process involved in realizing those achievements or performing those specific acts.

Do you want something to seem hard or difficult? Ok, then believe that it is so. Just because some things take more time or more effort to achieve, is this “hard”? Hard and difficult are disempowering unnecessary labels. Use them if you want. But know that it only serves to cause any weight to feel heavier, any hurdle to appear higher, and any achievement to appear more distant and unattainable.

Deep down it also serves to feed our pride by thinking that something we achieved was “hard” to accomplish. Believing that we achieved something “difficult” puffs us up and builds our self-esteem. The truth is that this is nothing more than a negative habit we have developed. Like any preprogrammed disempowering habit, we must become aware of it, question it, expose it, and then choose and decide to change and correct it.

Let me clarify that this empowerment rule does NOT ignore the fact that there may be good reasons to feel like some things DO seem "hard" to accomplish. This empowerment rule is NOT ignorant to the fact that we are prone to perceive some tasks as challenging, frustrating, difficult. It does NOT ignore that achieving some of our desires and goals may often seem hard to do. It does NOT negate the felt reality that in many situations we experience perceived struggle, challenges, difficulty, etc. And that much of the work we do may seem hard and back breaking whether physically, intellectually, or emotionally. This empowerment rule does not ignore ANY of that. What this empowerment rule DOES say, is that it is SUPPOSED to be EASY. It only seems hard because we are doing it wrong, or with the wrong attitude or mindset.

Let me give you a simple example; let's say that Tom has never played guitar and he attempts it for the first time. It will seem very hard for Tom to produce any sort of pleasing music out of the instrument. Is it because it is hard? No, it is because he is doing it WRONG. Because if you hand that same guitar to someone who knows how to play it, they will play it easily, and effortlessly. They can make it sing beautifully and with seeming ease.

So then, let me ask you, is playing the guitar easy or hard? The answer is, it is SUPPOSED to be easy. But, for it to become easy one must dedicate the time and practice to learn the EASY way to play the guitar. There is always an EASY WAY. We simply have to find it and then make our way in it.

"It seems hard because you are doing it wrong!"

I am not attempting some tricky word play here, but to establish that the empowered way to understand this is that we confuse "hard" with "wrong". We should accept that all things are supposed to be easy. Because once we develop the skill, we realize how easy it is. Easy is waiting for us to experience it. Easy is a state that already exists in the field of infinite potential. We simply have to make our way into it. Do you see it now?

We should expect and accept that anything we first attempt to do, we will likely do wrong. Because we have not yet trained ourselves to do it right. If on top of that we add a wrong attitude, then of course our experience of that reality will be one of "hard, frustrating, difficult, etc."

Doing it wrong seems hard. Doing it right feels easy. It is only hard because we are doing it wrong or with a wrong attitude. This is the bottom line. Therefore, we should resist using the negative labels of hard, difficult, etc. As they only serve to discourage us from achieving the easy state.

As I was explaining this empowerment rule to my youngest son, he was not convinced. He was skeptical and persisted in thinking that some things are just plain hard. He said "what if you are trying to pick up a very heavy weight, that is just hard". To which I replied that if, for example, you try and lift an elephant, this would of course seem very, very hard. But a person trying to lift an elephant is the wrong way to lift an elephant. You need to find the proper equipment that one could easily operate in order to lift the elephant. Then it would be easy (and fun).

You can apply this "Easy" way of thinking to anything you may perceive as "hard". Find the right tools, resources, skills, etc. in order for it to be easy. Because you can now accept this to be true. That since it is supposed to be easy then there must always be an easy way. And we just have to find it

It is often our very own mindset that creates the resistance. When we label something as hard or difficult WE are creating resistance and a negative perception of greater struggle. We should simply decide to resist LESS. We should decide to accept that it is supposed to be easy, and this is what we will eventually experience. You should continually put yourself into that mindset of ease and resistance less.

Furniture Movers

This reminds me of a wonderful invention called furniture movers. Furniture movers are small pads that you place under heavy furniture whenever you want to move the furniture from one spot to the other. Without the furniture movers, the resistance and friction created by the floor surface and the weight of the furniture makes moving the furniture very difficult. However, once you place the moving pads under the furniture they serve to reduce the friction of the two surfaces and you can now move very heavy furniture literally with one hand. It is easy.

The difference between the hard and easy experience was the difference in the friction between the two surfaces. We can liken our attitudes to the friction. When we are in a mindset of "difficult" or "hard" this creates unnecessary friction that causes the work load to seem much heavier. If we simply adopt a frictionless attitude by choosing to resist less, then the load will feel lighter. We can make it easier by simply choosing a different mindset. One of less resistance. An attitude that says, "it is supposed to be easy".

I often encounter conversations with people where the predominant words used are "difficult, hard, tough, challenging, pain in the butt", etc. This type of thinking and speech perpetuates the notion of "Hard". Just because it takes time and dedicated efforts to realize certain goals or to develop a particular skill. Why do we call this hard?

If you continually say to yourself "that is hard, this is going to be hard, boy, that is really difficult, how hard was that, etc." all you are doing is perpetuating this negative perception and thus creating this notion of struggle, effort, difficulty, and toil.

Please realize that this is simply a choice. When we change our mindset and our vocabulary, it will inevitably help us to realize more effortless and productive results. As we will be in a more positive and frictionless mindset. Also, you will be less likely to give up if you believe that it will eventually become easy or that you will eventually find the easier way.

Consider the world class athletes, world famous musicians, or highly skilled artists. They perform amazing, unbelievable feats, and they make it look easy. The beauty and awe that their performances evoke is the result of the wonderful ease and grace with which they perform their varied skills. They are demonstrating the path of least resistance and conservation of energy in their performances.

Yes, of course it took them time and dedicated practice. But you now see how easy and effortless it is for them. They trained their minds and bodies over time to be able to perform the task or skill easily. They have achieved mastery. The human body and mind have the marvelous ability to master anything, to find the way of least resistance. To make it easy.

Why did the world class athlete or virtuoso musician achieve the easy state? Because **it was supposed to be easy all along**. If anything, that can be achieved, can be made to look easy, then this is obvious proof that it was supposed to be easy all along.

***"Always think that what you have to do is easy,
if it is at all possible of being done.
Then you will not expend any more strength
than what is necessary.
If you think it is difficult,
you will spend many times more strength
than is actually required to perform it.
You simply waste strength"***
Emile Coue

Thinking and believing that something is hard is a limiting and disempowering mindset. Remember that our thinking and believing are all choices that we make. Whenever you feel like a thing is hard to achieve, you can simply choose to get into a different mindset. Yes, you can simply choose to remind yourself that it is supposed to be easy. With this empowered mindset you will find that this will become more real for you. Because what you focus on you find.

Are you not yet convinced? Well then let me appeal to the laws of nature. Let me remind you that there are two physical laws of effortlessness. The law of conservation of energy and the principle of least resistance. Together they basically state that energy is always conserved and finds the path of least resistance. So, the things that happen should tend to happen easily. Finding the path of least resistance so that the minimum amount of energy is always used in the process of attaining or achieving anything.

Since energy is neither created or destroyed there is a fixed amount. Then it follows that we should be always seeking the path of least resistance. Develop the confidence of knowing that there is always that easy path. The path of least resistance. Whether in our thinking or in our doing. All we must do is find and fall into that easy path.

In nature, we see this principle of least resistance. All water flows downstream, always finding the path of least resistance. In nature, we also witness incredible beauty and awesome power, but also ease, effortlessness, and a beautiful playfulness.

Nature does not seemingly struggle; it does what it does effortlessly. Look at the ocean, it does not toil as it powerfully manages to roll its majestic waves and bring in the tides. In fact, it seems to be doing it in an effortless, playful way. Look at a great forest. Every year it effortlessly sheds its leaves and brings them all back again every season. This takes a tremendous amount of energy, yet it happens effortlessly during every spring and fall. Without fail and without complaint.

Even our bodies are designed to work effortlessly and with ease. Our bodies easily perform the trillions of amazing cellular functions that keep us alive. As a matter of fact, when there is something wrong with our bodies we say that the person has a disease. A dis-ease, a lack of doing what it is supposed to do easily. You see, it is supposed to be easy.

We must make our way being confident and trusting that there is always a path of least resistance. And the path of least resistance must start in our own thinking, attitude, and mindset. We must cultivate the mindset that it is supposed to be easy. This sets us up in accordance with both the principle of least resistance and the law of conservation of energy. Both of these principles work in our favor when we apply this Empowerment rule that states, it is supposed to be easy.

This mindset of EASY introduces anticipation, hope, and confidence. It beckons us to step forward and encourages us to keep working towards realizing the easy way. We must use our creative faculty to place ourselves in a state where we do not mind the effort. Because we know it is bringing us closer to that effortless, easy state. That beautiful state of least resistance and conservation of energy. To the masterful state of making the difficult look easy, because it now IS.

If it seems hard, you are doing it wrong, or with the wrong attitude. Look to find an easier, more effective, more creative way to accomplish what you are doing. There is always a better way, an easier approach. Find that easy way. The path of least resistance. Make sure your mindset is positive and creative. In this way, whatever you are doing will seem more effortless. If it is something you love to do, or you are convinced should be effortless you will inevitably realize this as true and thus experience that very effect.

Think of making a long, four-hour road trip somewhere. This can be a very boring and tedious experience. For some people driving for four hours can be a very "hard" task. As most people are not used to driving for more than 20-30 minutes at a time. So, driving long distances can be an arduous experience.

However, if I tell you that you have just won a million dollars, but you must drive to a location that is four hours away to claim it. I guarantee that the drive will be filled with anticipation, joy, and excitement. It will be easy, effortless, and fun. This proves the power of having the right mindset.

If we put ourselves in the mindset that anything we have to do is supposed to be easy, then it will be so. This is what we will inevitably experience. We will be less prone to becoming discouraged. We will move forward with the certainty that as we continue we are getting closer to finding the EASY WAY that awaits us.

By embracing this mindset of easy, we will tend to resist less and therefore reduce the effort involved to achieve any particular thing. Remember that often the resistance is of our very own creation. We are supposed to go with the flow……like water.

Bruce Lee says: "You must be shapeless, formless, like water. When you pour water in a cup, it becomes the cup. When you pour water in a bottle, it becomes the bottle. When you pour water in a teapot, it becomes the teapot. Water can drip, and it can crash. Become like water my friend."

As you become more practiced at anything it becomes progressively easier. So, why does the practice have to seem hard? Practice easily. Make mistakes, easily, try it again with a mindset of "easy does it". And trust that every minute that you invest in practice is getting you closer to the easy way.

Remember, that the concepts of easy and hard are only labels that we chose to apply. Doing is doing. Whether we call something easy or hard is simply our choice. So, you ask yourself, do I want it to seem "Hard" or do I want it to be "Easy". You Choose!!!

Empowerment Rule #10

The Answer Is "YES"

"Life, nature, and God always answer 'Yes' to you. What are you asking for?"
Mark Victor Hansen

The word YES is the simplest, yet most powerful word in the entire English language. It is simple because it only has three letters and one syllable. It is powerful because it is the word of infinite potentiality.

"YES", is the word we most long to hear. It conveys an approval, a desire granted, a confirmation. It is the sweetest of all words as it is non-judgmental and accepting. "Yes" is a door opening. It promises all things, grants all things, and agrees with all things. The word "YES" is an endless stream selflessly pouring forth.

"Yes, is the answer, and you know that for sure. Yes, is surrender, you got to let it, you got to let it go"
John Lennon

"Yes" carries you away into the realm of infinite possibilities as it is the word of pure potentiality. To properly embrace and apply this empowerment rule, you must understand the concept of infinite potentiality.

Infinite Potentiality

Think of any "thing", like chair, table, car, etc. How many different varieties of these things can you imagine? The answer is, you can imagine an infinite number of varieties for any of these things. Yes, you can literally spend an infinity conjuring up different varieties of any of these concepts, and still never be able to imagine them all. You will never be able to exhaust the different versions that exists in the state of infinite potentiality for any particular thing or idea. The potential variations for any thing are infinite. Are they not?

We exist in a world of infinite potential. For every concept, idea, or imagining there is an infinite number of potential variations, permutations, and forms of expression. Whether they are concepts of actual things like; chair, table, house, car. Or whether it is situations and happenings. These all have an infinite number of potential styles, colors, designs, scenarios, etc. The potentiality in any thing, concept or idea is literally inexhaustible and infinite. Which is why for anything that you can imagine the answer is, "Yes".

Infinite potentiality is the reason why there can be and always will be a different, better version of any conceived thing. There will always be a 2.0 or a 3.0 version of anything that man can create. Because the only limitation is our imagination. And to that there is no limit.

We live in a world of INFINITE POTENTIALITY. Where the possibilities are LIMITLESS. And it is through the means of our imagination that we have access to this realm of infinite possibilities. Our imagination is the key that unlocks that door.

"When you have exhausted all possibilities, remember this—you haven't."
Thomas Edison

Not only can we conceive of infinite possibilities, but we also have the capabilities and resources available to make them real. With the combination of our human ingenuity and the available natural and man-made resources, anything is possible. Because anything at all that you can imagine you can also, to some degree, realize. And therefore, the answer is always "Yes".

"Whatever the mind of man can conceive and believe it can achieve"
Napoleon Hill

Interestingly, as we discussed in the earlier chapter on the conscious and subconscious mind, "Yes" also happens to be the only word that your subconscious mind knows. Because it does not acknowledge the difference between something real or imagined. It knows that anything imagined can become realized and materialized. So, it simply does not bother with this distinction of materiality, since it is plugged in to and connected to the universal field of infinite possibility and potentiality.

The subconscious mind knows that all possibilities exist in the invisible realm. And that the only differences are vibrational frequencies. A thought has a particular vibrational frequency, as does the materialized image or thing. The difference is only in the degrees of their respective vibrational frequencies. Therefore, it always answers "YES" because it accepts that every potentiality is possible.

Quantum theory also bears out this notion of infinite potential as it aims to explain how the most fundamental stuff of the universe behaves. It has been discovered that the fundamental "stuff" that the universe is made of (subatomic particles) is simply energy potential and wave probabilities.

This "stuff" is not really "stuff" at all. It is essentially waves of information and energy that appear to exist not in fixed predictable states, but in a magic dance of probabilities and pure potentiality.

Yes, the very fiber of our reality, the material that is woven into the cloth of our objective experiences is nothing more than an infinite sea of energy and information that displays infinite potentiality as it is responsive to our intentions and observations.

The Reason for Infinite Possibilities

There is a rational and practical reason why infinite potentiality is a sheer necessity. The reason why there is infinite potential is simply because…perfection cannot be attained.

Yes, in this life, in our current existence, perfection is unattainable. And it is this very limitation. This inability to express, realize, or experience perfection that makes infinite possibilities not only possible, but necessary.

If the perfect chair could be realized, it would be unnecessary and impractical for any other variation to exist. Because once you have realized the "perfect" thing, any additional variability would be pointless and unnecessary. It would be a certain degradation. In the perfect state there is no need for variability or possibilities as perfection is immutable. And…. perfect!!

The universe in its transcendent wisdom offers us infinite potential as the necessary trade off to the inability to achieve perfection. Since we cannot achieve or experience perfection, it provides us the next best thing…infinite potential yielding infinite possibilities.

While we all instinctively know that perfection is not attainable in our current state, we also have a certain sense that perfection does exist. Simply because we can conceive of the concept, we know that it must be out there somewhere. Otherwise we would not be able to consciously consider it, so we trust that it is real.

We are not capable of comprehending the concept of perfection. Like the concept of infinity. We can accept that these concepts are real, but they are beyond our minds ability to grasp and understand their full significance.

Isn't it fascinating that as human beings we can actually conceive of concepts that are far beyond our ability to fully comprehend? Concepts like infinity, eternity, perfection. This must point to a greater mind out there somewhere, does it not? When faced with these far-out concepts that we can on the one hand grasp but on the other hand never fully understand, the best we can do is trust they are real, and marvel at them in curious awe and wonder.

"Some truths
(like the incomprehensible concept of infinity)
can only be accepted and admired;
they can't be condensed and wrapped in a package
that fits inside the human brain"
John McArthur

The Impossibility of Attaining Perfection

Mathematics is a universal language that bridges all other languages. It is the language of the universe, as it is used to calculate and quantify the features and forces of the universe as we understand them. Since mathematics is the language of the universe, and the universe has infinite potential, then it must follow that mathematics should have an infinite vocabulary. A vocabulary that is capable of infinite expression. And we find that it does. Because there is an infinity of numbers. Not only is there an infinite number of numbers, but even in between the smallest numbers we also find infinity.

For instance, how many numbers are there between 0 and 1? The answer is, an infinite number. Let's make the gap even smaller. How many numbers are there between 0 and .0001? Again, the answer is, an infinite number. This is mind boggling, but it is true. There is infinity in the space between any two numbers. Mathematics is the vocabulary of the infinite. It illustrates and confirms this magnificent truth that the universe has infinite potentiality.

"Number rules the universe" is the ruler of forms and ideas, and the cause of gods and demons"
Pythagoras

So, let us now use mathematics, the vocabulary of the universe, to help us better understand the impossibility of attaining perfection (in our current reality). Let's propose that the mathematical equation for perfection is 100%, 100% of the time. If something that is measurable and quantifiable can maintain a state of 100%, 100% of the time, then it could rightly be called "perfect". However, in anything that we can observe, measure or keep score of, we have not been able to witness this phenomenon of perfection. This mathematical impossibility of 100%, 100% of the time without fail or slightest fluctuation. This state is simply not sustainable in any natural situation or worldly condition.

Here is a very simple example to help illustrate the impossibility of achieving perfection. Let's say you attempt to shoot a perfect number of basketball free-throws. You make the first 7 in a row…you are now at 100%. But you miss the next throw. You are now 7 of 8. Which is less than perfect.

Let me ask you, how many more perfect throws would you need to make in order to get back to 100%? The shocking but true answer is, that even if you could make an INFINITE number of perfect free throws from that point forward, you would NEVER be able to once again achieve perfection. Mathematically you would never again be able to get to 100%. You see, once you fall from the perfect state (100%) you can never again attain it.

The reality is that in life, we have all "missed a free throw". Meaning that we all, in every area of our lives, have somehow fallen short of perfection. We have all done, thought, or said things that have rightly qualified us as less than perfect. If we are honest, we know this to be true. And if we deceive ourselves by saying that we haven't, then we are less than perfectly honest.

"The best of men are but men at best"
Unknown

The reason perfection is not within our grasp in this existence is because there exists a powerful and mysterious force that, like gravity, is always at work. This mysterious force, that can be better understood by studying the concept of entropy, is perpetually acting on all the stuff of the universe. It is the law of constant deterioration, degradation, and decomposition. It is the universal law of constant undoing. Continually causing all things to move towards a state of chaos and disorder.

It is this very law that produces the ever-present headwind that prevents us from attaining perfection. It is this force that creates that slight, yet infinite, unbreachable chasm between our current state and the utopian, unreachable state of perfection.

This mysterious force of constant undoing is present in everything and in every millisecond of time. It is mysteriously woven into the very fabric of our existence. Perpetually "breaking down" all things, both visible and invisible. Continually preventing the state of perfection from being attained.

The very instant that something is created it starts to succumb to the process of deterioration. All things new immediately start to become old. All systems move inexorably towards disorder. This is the natural tendency for all things in our realm of existence.

It is this law of disorder and deterioration that makes work necessary. As nothing left alone ever becomes cleaner, newer, more organized. Just the opposite is true. Anything left alone will inevitably deteriorate, tending towards disorder and the loss of energy (entropy).

We must continually apply work (energy) to bring order back into all the natural systems and things in our realm of existence. Because they all are all subject to this mysterious force. This tendency towards disorder that pervades all physical existence. It is because of the effects of this law that we must continually do work.

The next time you organize your closet or drawers, know that you are undoing the effect of this law. Your closet, if left untended will eventually become a pile of disordered, disheveled clothes. Long hair, if never combed will naturally become more and more messy and tangled. Your garden if not tended and cared for will become a wild mess of weeds. These are simple examples of the law of disorder and degradation having its effect.

It is this very law that prevents us from achieving perfection. It creates that subtle yet infinite space between our current existence and a state of perfection. Yet it is this very condition that makes infinite possibilities possible. You see, without the effects of this mysterious force, we would experience perfection and thus have no need for possibilities. The attainment of perfection would make the concept of possibilities unnecessary. Think about it, what would be the point of entertaining any other possibility if perfection could be attained?

We exist in a condition of imperfection. This is important to accept and embrace, as believing otherwise would be delusional and false. However, this understanding should not cause to demotivate or discourage you. But, instead, to encourage and inspire you to always pursue getting better. To always seek to grow in any area you desire and intend.

You are not perfect, you will never be perfect, but you have infinite potential. And, no matter how much you may grow or improve in any area, you can still always become infinitely better.

Therefore, you should always press forward. Moving continually towards realizing the best version of you. Defining your best self by way of the empowerment rules and principles presented in this book.

So, take a deep breath and accept the following. Perfection is unattainable in this current existence. But, what we have in its place is infinite possibilities and potential. What a wonderful alternative.

It is said that the purpose of man is to grow, just like it is the purpose of plants, and all living things to grow. We are purposed to keep growing as long as we are alive. And so, it is our calling to keep getting better. To keep reaching further. To continually move towards our perfecting. Pressing forward and realizing our infinite potential. It is this calling to keep reaching further that serves the purpose of both, a testimony to our capacity for continued growth, and the infinite possibilities that this life provides for us.

Things can always get better. YOU can always be better. There is always an opportunity to improve in any number of ways and the universe is calling you to this end. It is offering you infinite possibilities. Which is why the answer is “YES”. Because anything imagined can be realized and objectified.

Infinite Possibility Eliminates DOUBT

Trust and have faith in whatever it is that you set your heart and mind to. Why would you doubt when you know that all possibilities are possible? And, you have the power to choose. This knowledge should fill you with hope and cause you to be confident.

As such, doubt should have no place in your life. As doubt is the absence of faith. It is doubt that plants the seeds of failure and disillusionment in your life. It robs you of your joy and confidence. Doubt must be removed and retired. It must be banished to the mountain heap of useless and limiting ideals and mindsets. You have no use for it. Because your answer is "YES".

This is encouraging and EMPOWERING. It should cause you to take heart and always look forward with hope, confidence, and anticipation.

In this life, you will never be perfect, so be kind to yourself and don't judge too harshly. But know and trust that you can be infinitely better. So, continue to grow in any and every way you determine and desire. Become more patient, understanding, positive, confident, gracious, encouraging, informed, aware, capable, determined, skilled, etc. Never stop growing, learning, and becoming more. The universe beckons you and is ready to say "YES".

In this life all possibilities exist. By your focus and attention, you draw to yourself that which you have chosen. What you focus on you will find. Your intentionality determines your potentiality, there is infinite potential and…. The answer is YES!!

In Closing...

Now that you have read the 10 Rules of Empowerment and the accompanying Empowerment Habits, what happens next? Well, if you agreed with and accepted any of the rules, principles, or habits covered in this book, then it is my hope that you will endeavor to apply them to your thinking and to your doing. That you will choose to see your life as the ultimate "do it yourself" project and thus become inspired to continually pursue the best version of you. Your Empowered Self.

"Act well your part, there all the honor lies"
Alexander Pope

You are unique, you are special, you are important. You are already a masterpiece. But remember that you are also a work in progress. You have been called to realize the fullness of your potential. The universe beckons you to become the best version of you. To continually realize your infinite potential. This is your highest purpose. And only you are uniquely qualified for this very task.

Also remember that you have an audience. Your friends, family, coworkers, etc. They all want and deserve to see your BEST. They are secretly cheering you on to deliver your best performance. To become the best YOU that only YOU can be.

I encourage you to persevere in taking the concepts covered in the Empowerment rules and make them an integral part of your mental programming. They must become the new paradigms; the updated software that will produce for you new, more empowered outputs. New thinking, that will produce new feelings, that will cause new actions, creating new habits that will yield new results.

Persevere to work out your empowerment. Consciously and continuously ask yourself as you make your way along; "what empowerment principles apply to this situation? And what habit must I develop or implement in this area of my life to effectively apply these new empowerment beliefs?

"Sow a thought and you reap an action;
sow an act and you reap a habit;
sow a habit and you reap a character;
sow a character and you reap a destiny"
Ralph Waldo Emerson

It is helpful to understand this last quote in reverse:

Your destiny is determined by your character.
Your character is determined by your habits.
Your habits are determined by your actions.
Your actions are determined by your thoughts.

So, as YOU intentionally determine and direct your thoughts, you are determining and directing your DESTINY. And now is the time for you to intentionally define your destiny by application of the Empowerment Rules and Habits contained in this book.

Become Extra Ordinary

Becoming extra ordinary may sound like a tall order, but when you break it down you will find that it is simply achieved by making very small adjustments. You see, we all start with ordinary…which is what we all are, ordinary. There is only ONE other ingredient we must add to our ordinary state and this is a little dash of "EXTRA". Yes, just a small "extra" in everything you do will, by definition, make you Extra-Ordinary.

You must always be wanting and willing to find and to do those little extras in every area of your life. It is really just that simple. And doing so will thus define you as Extra ordinary. So, always keep the door of your consideration open to finding those little extras that you can apply all along the way as you move forward in your life.

It is my hope that in the pages of this book you have found new information or information that reinforces key things you already knew. That will inspire and enable you to find and do those little extras in every area of your life.

Always remember that at first any change seems "hard". This is because you may not have clear intentions or right attitudes. And because you have not yet harnessed the power of precedent. You need time and persistence to weave those little "extras" into the fabric of your subconscious programming and conditioned actions. As you persevere you will find that becoming extraordinary is no tall order at all. But simply a series of intentional, persistent, incremental steps. But that will yield an amazing result.

Now is the time to act, to define yourself by what you do. Commit to self-mastery. The journey starts today, right here, right now. Where you stand. Every day and every moment becomes the starting point from which you should move forward. You must be determined to never stop on this journey of empowerment. Take baby steps or bold steps, but, always commit to moving forward. This is your own, unique, individual journey, and you have the rest of your life to experience it.

Life, The Ultimate Olympic Event

We are all engaged in an Olympic event called life. Every morning you wake up and it is “game on” whether you are in “shape” or not. Whether you have “trained” or not. Whether you are ready or not, you must compete in this Olympic event that cannot be put off. This daily race that cannot be avoided. This contest that cannot be forfeited. When the bell sounds every morning, it is GAME ON!!! There is no snooze button on life.

Since life is the ultimate Olympic event and the challenges are quite formidable. You must be well trained. Continually working on becoming the most prepared, most mentally “in the game” and most fit to succeed. Think about an Olympic athlete. Their mindset, training, and conditioning must all be at the highest level. World class. They are constantly pushing for improvement and pressing towards bettering their last, best performance.

It should be no different for us all. As we are all engaged in the ultimate Olympic event called LIFE. Participation is not optional, you either play to win or plan to lose. Choosing to play or not to play is not an option. What you can choose are the attitudes, actions, and responses that will determine your level of success or failure.

As in any competition, to succeed you must be aware of the rules, and become trained in the skills and strategies that will enable you to win. The information shared in this book provides you the key principles, rules, mindsets, and habits that will enable you to compete at that WORLD CLASS level.

“Remember, life is just a game,
and no one gets out alive”
David Lee Roth

You must cultivate the attitude of a champion. The heart of a warrior, the mindset of a Winner. You must be willing to live Boldly. Because, remember, in this Olympic event called daily living, no one gets out alive. Since you cannot take anything with you and you know how this all ends. What is the point of holding back, of giving less than all you have to give? Yes, the only logical response is to be willing to go all in. To double down. To leave it all on the field.

The Triathlon of Life

Your Relationships
Your Work
Your Self

In order to truly succeed and realize your full empowerment, you must be committed to continually improving, growing, and winning in each of the three areas that comprise your life.

#1. Your Relationships

"The best feeling in the world is knowing that you actually mean something to someone"

Our accomplishments and experiences are void and meaningless unless they are couched in the context of relationships. If we are not able to share our joys, sorrows, successes, and struggles we miss out on the most delicious part of life. For it is in the sharing of our experiences that they become truly significant and more enjoyable. The wonderful experiences when shared, become even more wonderful.

On the other hand, when we are able to share our sorrows and frustrations they become easier for us to bear. Everything we experience in life becomes more meaningful and special as we get the opportunity to share it with someone else. Especially with our friends and loved ones.

You must see your relationships as opportunities to grow by your willingness to give more and be more towards others. Desire to become someone that always positively impacts the lives of all those you interact with in every situation.

By being intentional you can make your relationships the most that they can be. In your relationships you must be giving and understanding. Always applying rule #4 Give to Get. Remember that you have an audience, and your audience wants to see you at your very best. They deserve the best version of you. They deserve your best performance.

Everything you do and achieve is ultimately in the context of your relationships. They are important because in large part, the quality of your relationships determines the quality of your life.

The foundation of your thinking in every relationship must be established by asking; What is my role and purpose in this relationship? And the answer to this question, in every situation, is that you are here to benefit and bless the other person in the unique way that only you can.

We must be faithful stewards in our relationships. You must see every relationship as special and important. And everyone you interact with as worthy of receiving the very best you have to offer. Value all the people in your life and always persevere to make them feel **important and appreciated.**

#2. Your Work

"You can't have a million-dollar dream on a minimum wage work ethic"

It is in your work, whatever that may be, that you have a unique opportunity to realize your potential for achievement. To hone and apply your faculties, unique skills, and capabilities in the pursuit of organizational objectives.

It is in our work setting where we find the most structure and the most directed intentionality. As every organization is set up in very intentional ways for the very specific purposes of furthering the best interests of the organization and towards succeeding in that particular field.

Work allows you the opportunity to find your place in this structured enterprise to apply all your talents for the purpose of adding value and championing the cause of your organization. You will find many opportunities for growth and development in the context of work and as such, you must embrace and welcome those opportunities.

Many people resent their work, this is a very negative, defeating, and disempowering mindset. You must embrace and honor your work, whatever it may be, as it provides for your livelihood. As such you must persevere to always work to the very best of your abilities. You must do meaningful, earnest, effective, and productive work. Where the details matter and your intentionality is to always deliver above what is expected.

You should always be inclined to **learn more, care more, and do more** in the organization that employs you. Or in the business that you have developed. Having this mindset calls out your Empowered self.

#3. Yourself

"It's hard to keep that which has not been obtained through personal development"
Jim Rohn

And lastly, you must be committed to yourself. To taking care of and nurturing your body, mind, and spirit. Because if you don't take care of yourself who will? You cannot be your Empowered Self and inspire or benefit others if you are not at your personal best.

You must be strong in your body, mind, and spirit, so that you can set an empowering example and become a source of inspiration to yourself and to others. People are always looking to be inspired and to find someone they can admire. Let that someone be you.

"Work harder on yourself than you do at your job"
Jim Rohn

You must be mindful of your diet. Eating to live and not living to eat. Remembering that the foods you eat will ultimately serve one of two purposes, to heal you or hurt you. Become informed on food and nutrition and let that information help shape your eating habits rather than eating out of convenience and prior conditioning. Be mindful and intentional in your eating as your health and wellbeing depend on it.

"Let thy medicine be thy food and thy food be thy medicine."
Hippocrates (father of medicine)

Also remember that your body is designed for movement, not for stagnation. So, learn about the different forms of exercise and determine what specific exercise routines will best serve to keep your body limber, conditioned, and strong. You must develop some form of physical exercise routine and stick to it. Even if you vary it as your interest levels change.

"Take care of your body.
It's the only place you have to live"
Jim Rohn

You must also exercise your mind. Feed it positive constructive information. Read books on topics that interest you. Seek out instructional or inspirational videos to feed you mind and continually expand your knowledge in any area you choose. Avoid the overconsumption mindless forms of entertainment as this only serves to dull your mind.

Make it a daily practice to set aside 5-10 minutes every day for quiet contemplation, meditation, or prayer. As this connects and centers you from the inside out, rather than always being stimulated and influenced from the outside in.

This daily practice should include; thinking about your intentions in the three areas of your life, numbering through your goals, objectives, and desires. Setting that mental picture of the things you long to achieve or experience, and of the person you choose to become. Also use this time for gratitude. To think about the many things or people in your life you are grateful for. This daily practice of contemplation is food for your spirit. Find a practice that suits you and stick to it.

Mind Your Habits:

"A nail is driven out by another nail.
Habit is overcome by habit."
Desiderate Erasmus

We are all creatures of habit. Over time we have formed our own unique patterns of thinking, feeling, speaking, and acting. These habits, for the most part, define who we are and, consequently, what we can achieve.

Sadly, most of the habits that define you have been forged without your conscious direction or intention. Yes, for the most part, you have become a product of your own unconscious conditioning. Unintentionally programmed to respond and behave in ways that may not always suit your higher purposes or deepest desires.

Many of your habits have been born out of inattention or wrong thinking. It is your very own unconscious programming and the resulting habits they produce that are the source of much of the discontent, frustration, and disempowerment you may currently be experiencing.

"My actions are ruled by
appetite, passion, prejudice, greed,
love, fear, environment, habit,
and the worst of these tyrants is habit.
Therefore, if I will be a slave to habit
let me be a slave to good habits.
My bad habits must be destroyed
and new furrows prepared for good seed"
Og Mandino

With the information you have learned in this book you can develop a new and more empowered mindset that will enable you to intentionally determine the new empowered habits that will serve to form the fabric of your new personality. They will define the new YOU. Your Empowered Self.

"Be as you wish to seem"
Socrates

Empowerment has a short and a long game, you have to be willing to play both well. The short game is the daily application of the habits and disciplines that will produce the results that you desire. The long game is to continue to soak up the principles and truths of empowerment so that they increasingly become your default mental programming. Thus, causing new empowered habits and actions to come more effortlessly. Since the underlying programming has been embraced at your deepest subconscious level. You will then, more and more, automatically respond in ways consistent with the rules of empowerment.

Ultimately, who we are is evidenced by our actions. The world says, "show me". Talk is cheap, but actions are gold. Information must be applied and acted on for it to have its proper effect. As Einstein says, "Nothing happens until something moves". In everything it is not that we can't, but that we don't. So…

"Prove your words by your deeds"
Seneca The Younger

You now begin a journey of living a more purposeful, intentional, empowered life. This becomes a lifelong endeavor that begins now. And will extend to every "now" that you find yourself in. As your life is a constant succession of nows.

You now realize that everything starts with a mindset. With the right empowered mindset your thoughts start to move you through this mysterious process of realizing from the invisible to the visible in every area of your life. And you will start to materialize to varying degrees the very real and positive effects of your new Empowered mindset.

***"Excellence is an art won by training and habituation.
We do not act rightly because we have
virtue or excellence, but rather we have those
because we have acted rightly.
We are what we repeatedly do.
Excellence, then, is not an act
but a habit."***
Aristotle

You are a unique and marvelous work of art created by the Master Craftsman of the Universe. The same hand that sculpted the Universe is the one that has carefully crafted you. You are not an accident, you are His PURPOSED creation. Your core intentionality has been seeded by His very own sovereign purpose. This means that your true I Am has been purposed by Him. And this is the spark that ignites your unique being. Therefore, you are purposed to shine bright in all you do. Reflecting HIS magnificent glory as you were thus intended.

May the information in this book inspire and enable you to reveal your inner champion, your best self.... **YOUR EMPOWERED SELF**!!!

The 10 Rules of Empowerment

Only YOU stand in the way of YOU

If YOU want things to change YOU have to change

If YOU want things to get better YOU have to get Better

YOU have to Give to Get

YOU have the Power to Choose

What YOU focus on YOU Will find

YOUR intentionality Determines YOUR potentiality

YOU can achieve anything YOU desire believe and ACT on

It is supposed to be Easy

The answer is YES

YOU are not
Power- less
YOU Are
Power FULL

Y.E.S.

Made in the USA
Las Vegas, NV
27 June 2022

50787864R00152